A BOY

back from

HEAVEN

A BOY
back from
HEAVEN

Celeste *and* Matthew Goodwin

PLAIN SIGHT PUBLISHING
An Imprint of Cedar Fort, Inc.
Springville, UT

ISBN 13: 978-1-4621-1385-9

Published by Plain Sight Publishing, an imprint of Cedar Fort, Inc.
2373 W. 700 S., Springville, UT 84663
Distributed by Cedar Fort, Inc., www.cedarfort.com

   Library of Congress Cataloging-in-Publication Data on file.

Cover design by Angela D. Baxter
Cover design © 2014 by Lyle Mortimer
Edited and typeset by Whitney Lindsley

Printed in the United States of America

10 9 8 7 6 5 4 3 2 1

Printed on acid-free paper

᪥

F or Matthew and Conner. Thank you for teaching me what unconditional love truly is. You are amazing children who are loved beyond measure. The world became a better place the day each of you was born.

CONTENTS

ACKNOWLEDGMENTS

I n the years since 2007, our personal lives have been filled with change, renewal, growth, and understanding. As I have watched my children grow not only physically but also spiritually, I have come to appreciate the little things. I am learning to put things into perspective, and I am evolving, not only as a mother but also as a human being. It has been a gift beyond measure.

One of the greatest blessings God has placed in our lives is amazing family and friends. Without these valuable relationships built around love, I honestly don't know how we would have made it through some of the darkest days of our lives. It goes without saying that there are far too many to name each of them individually. To every person that has offered up prayers for and words of comfort to our family, we are forever thankful to you. Our gratitude is immeasurable, and you have helped teach our children what caring and compassion looks like.

INTRODUCTION

Has your faith ever been tested? Insurmountable events can make even the strongest believers question what they've always been taught about God. *Trust in God for He will not give you more than you can handle.* These words are meant to give us hope in times of trial. Often they can be a source of comfort and faith. Parents often experience tribulations that comes with caring for our children. It's during these times that we turn our trust toward God and understand he has a plan set for us. However, when we are faced with unavoidable obstacles, it is often easy to question God's will. Even when we cannot see the light, we must remember that God is walking with us. He has a plan, and we must trust. This story is a testament of what it means to put blind faith and the life of your child in God's hands. It is the account of a courageous little boy who walked the path to heaven and taught each of us the amazing love of God. We cannot know the unbearable journeys that are set before us, but we can trust that God will see us through them.

one

IT ALL CHANGED

April 2, 2007, was an absolutely stunning spring day in South Louisiana. The trees were in full bloom with life burgeoning everywhere. It was a perfect day for Matthew's preschool class to have their annual Easter party, a day filled with egg hunts, picnics, and playing with friends. But instead of searching for eggs, Matthew was continuing the nearly weeklong battle for his young life in the pediatric intensive care unit of a Baton Rouge hospital after a routine outpatient surgery to have tubes placed in his ears went terribly awry. I decided to open the curtain that morning and let a little sunlight in the window of his dark hospital room. What a wonderfully gorgeous day God had given us. The beauty that shone outside was a far cry from the black cloud that would loom over that room in a few hours.

Matthew's face was still pale, and his eyes had deep, dark circles under them; but for the first time in days we could see a glimpse of his little soul back in his eyes. He was exhausted and weak, but I assured him we were getting closer to finding some answers and getting him better. It was astoundingly difficult to give him this assurance when I wasn't totally convinced myself.

After getting our two-year-old, Conner, settled in at my parent's house, my husband, Billy, returned to the hospital early that morning. We knew this would be a day of change, hopefully for the better, as we looked for answers about Matthew's health problems. As promised by our conversation the previous evening, Matthew's PICU physicians had consulted with Children's Hospital in New Orleans. His condition was explained, and their findings to date were shared. It was agreed that he should indeed be transferred for more specialized care and treatment. Over the past week, his condition had continued to decline at a rapid pace, so his doctors were working feverishly to understand why his body was being ravaged by uncontrolled blood pressures. The dangerously elevated blood pressures threatened to take his life at any moment. Time was of the essence.

As the morning wore on, it became clear that Matthew's state was getting critical. A trauma nurse from Children's Hospital would be accompanying him on an ambulance ride to New Orleans, but before his transfer, the staff needed to take care of a couple of things. First, he needed to have his arterial line repositioned in order for it to render accurate blood pressure readings directly from his artery. Additionally, the doctors decided to place a central line in his groin. This was not going to be the most pleasant procedure to have done, but it would eliminate the need to have IVs constantly placed. With the life-threatening blood pressures his body had experienced, it was nearly impossible to keep an IV in place. The bedside procedure to reposition the arterial line and place the central line would be much different than what he had experienced a few days ago. He would again be sedated, but this time the nurses would gently ask me and Billy to step out for a bit.

Matthew's godmother, Dawn, had called before the procedure and said she would head to the hospital and bring food. I was so grateful for this gesture but knew there was no way I could eat. Her presence and comfort was gift enough. Once the final prayers were said, we were allowed to stay just long enough for the sedation to take effect. Before he went to sleep, Billy and I each kissed Matthew and told him how much we loved him.

As soon as Matthew was asleep, we walked out of that room. It was a walk filled with much foreboding. We felt so much apprehension in leaving him. I knew that he was in great hands, but the sense of a looming catastrophe could not be shaken. My intuition said something was just not right. The gravity of just how sick Matthew was hung with me and made my heart very heavy.

This feeling had been present every day for the past week, but this day was different. Different how? Different why? I didn't know. All I did know was the spring day's serenity that was uplifting just a few hours earlier was replaced by a sense of dread and uncertainty. We knew the danger of his extremely high blood pressure. Some readings reached as high as 240 systolic over 140 diastolic. A normal reading for a four-year-old boy should be around 90 systolic over 60 diastolic. This was potentially deadly even for an adult.

We feared that he could suffer a stroke or heart attack. What if he slipped into a coma?

The look on Billy's face as we waited for the procedure to be over was reminiscent of the worried look he had in the days leading up to Matthew's tonsillectomy. The anxiety built, and I could take it no longer. We headed back upstairs to the PICU to at least see if they were finished repositioning the arterial line and placing the central line. We entered the PICU on the opposite side of where Matthew's room was located. The information nurse said they were not quite through, but it would be completed soon. She promised to let us go in just as soon as it was all done.

I didn't want only to see and hold my baby, I *needed* to be with him. It was an unexplained feeling of urgency. Finally, she let us in. We nearly sprinted across the unit. Walking into his room this time was much different from any time the past week. Even though the procedure was successfully completed and transfer could begin after he was awake, the dread was still present for some reason. He was still unconscious from the sedation, and the nurses assured us he should be waking up any minute. I told myself that this sense of foreboding would be lifted once he woke up. Soon Matthew did wake up, and he seemed more like "our Matthew" than he had seemed in a week! What a relief. Or so it should have been. We spent the next few minutes talking about the trip New Orleans and the cool ambulance ride he would take with his daddy. Suddenly his eyes rolled back into his head, and the minutes that followed would forever change every aspect of our lives.

His eyes, heart, and mind would see things that few get to experience in this lifetime. He walked the path to Jesus and received an affirmation of just who our guardian angels are and a confirmation that God does indeed hear our prayers. His experience would raise a question no parent is ever prepared to answer: "Mommy, does that mean I died?"

two

THE BEGINNING

Billy and I never discussed "if" we wanted children. We understood this was a calling we had in our hearts. We often brought up the topic of children in many of our conversations. Since we were both in our late twenties when we married, we felt like there was no need to delay the start of our family. In November 2000 I found out that I was pregnant with our first child. I was overcome by happiness and fear all at the same time. I was born to be a mother, but I was also terrified at the thought of getting it wrong. But more than anything, I couldn't wait to tell Billy. We spent the holidays dreaming of how exciting it was going to be the following Christmas with our little one crawling around. By January, I was nearing the end of the first trimester of pregnancy.

I woke up one chilly morning with the feeling that something just was not right. After praying that this was not the case, I made a call to my obstetrician. By 2:00 p.m. that afternoon, our dreams of becoming parents had been crushed. It wasn't in God's plan for us yet. The ultrasound showed that the baby hadn't grown after six weeks. A D&C was scheduled for the next week. While recovering a few days after the procedure, I got a phone call and was informed that the pregnancy had been a partial molar pregnancy. We were urged not to start trying again right away. We were advised to wait several months, but by early April we could try again. This would be one of God's many lessons to teach me patience. Parenthood took longer than anticipated, and we were beginning to wonder if it was indeed what God would want for us.

three

MATTHEW EMORY GOODWIN

Almost everyone you talk to can tell you exactly where they were on the morning of September 11, 2001. I recall that morning vividly. It was a gorgeous day. I was at work, and it was a rather quiet morning. I remember a good friend of mine coming into my office to say that her husband had just called to say that a plane had hit one of the towers in New York. In an instant, our way of life as United States citizens changed. I spent the day monitoring the news and the events transpiring and sending prayers of protection for all of those affected. I didn't really understand the magnitude of it until I got home from work that afternoon. I turned on the TV and remember watching in disbelief the terrible events of that tragic morning unfold.

Late September brought even more devastation into our lives. I learned that my uncle Ned was not doing well and would soon be called home. When the call came at the end of the month saying he had passed, we felt completely empty. Uncle Ned was like a grandfather to me, and I was horribly devastated to lose someone so precious. His presence always brought a sense of calm and happy. Uncle Ned and Aunt Louise had been ever present in my family's life. A six-hundred-mile gap in addresses never stopped them from sharing in the good and bad times. After the miscarriage, the first call I got was from Uncle Ned telling me how much he loved me and that everything would work out in the right time.

So much had taken place over those few weeks. Billy and I were both emotionally drained. In the "trying to get pregnant" department, we just knew that this would definitely not be the month. We had experienced too much stress and drama for me to even concentrate on getting pregnant.

However, we should never question God's timing. Great news came in October 2001 that I was again pregnant. Who would have thought? It felt different this time. It felt real. During the second trimester, an ultrasound showed it was a boy. We felt the most overwhelming feeling that there was great purpose to the life that would soon join our world. It was as though there was a constant wave of peace. That's all we needed. We started planning for the nursery and scheduled the shower.

Matthew Emory would be our firstborn. We took great consideration when trying to find the absolute perfect name. None of the names thrown out ever seemed to fit. Then, one morning—just like it was sent directly from the heavens—his name came to us. Matthew! That was it. It was perfect! During the eighth month, the early contractions started, which began several trips to the obstetrician and the first in a string of ultrasounds. I now think Matthew must be the world record holder for ultrasounds because they started before he even entered the world.

One ultrasound revealed that his amniotic fluid was dangerously low. We started looking at options to see how early he could safely be delivered. At thirty-four weeks, he decided to turn breech and not turn back around. At thirty-five weeks he decided to stop moving. This landed us an overnight stay in the hospital. He wouldn't respond to the attempts of maternal fetal medicine to "startle" him with their bullhorn. By early the next week, I was in my obstetrician's office yet again, and he said that at this point

Matthew was safer being delivered than trying to make it to his due date. My C-section was scheduled for the next morning at seven.

At 7:25 a.m. on June 12, 2002, God placed Matthew Emory Goodwin in our lives weighing in at six pounds twelve ounces. He measured nineteen and three-quarters inches long. Perfect! Finally, our angel was here in our arms. At this moment I felt what God's perfect and unending love could mean. How could we love some-one we just laid eyes on? It was effortless when we marveled in the work of this miracle sent straight from God into our arms. Even though he was delivered four weeks early, he was thriving. He was breathing on his own, so there was no need for the NICU.

All of his grandparents, aunts, uncles, nannies, and friends shared in the joy. We were so grateful that Matthew would know all four of his grandparents. His Maw Maw and Ghe Ghe along with Nana and Paw Paw were ready to welcome this sweet baby with open arms. Because I had only memories of my maternal grand-mother, Grandma Massey, I always prayed for my children to truly know their grandparents. I loved my grandmother so much, and I lost her when I was fourteen. When Matthew was born, I wished Grandma Massey was still here so that she could see this beautiful baby. I wished she could hold him and allow Matthew to feel the love her hands always gave to those she touched.

Billy and I had a feeling of euphoria when we looked into the eyes of this amazing little miracle God had created. I knew instantly that I had just done what I was put on this earth to do: become a mom. Staring into his beautiful little eyes was surreal. Looking back, we had no way to protect him from the journey that awaited him before his fifth birthday. God had other plans in store for him, plans that included seeing the most beautiful sight imaginable and being able to share it.

four

SO IN LOVE

L ife got easier with each day. We were so in love with this little being. I felt changed, and it was awesome. Even through the sleepless nights, parenthood was the best. Billy was meant to be a daddy, and to see him bond with his son made me love him so much more. These bonds would prove to be so important in keeping our family together during the rough times ahead.

Our new life had begun as a family of three. We settled into family life quite nicely. Over the months, Matthew grew right on track. When it came to his health and development, he was "normal" in every way, and I always gave thanks that Matthew was as healthy as he was.

Watching that baby grow into each new phase over the next couple of years was remarkable. The overwhelming feeling of this child having great purpose when I was pregnant never waned. It only became more intense after he was born. As I would rock him, he would stare intently at me with beautiful eyes. His eyes conveyed so much love and peace. It always felt to us that Matthew was the one doing the teaching instead of the other way around. Billy attended Catholic school, and I was baptized in the Catholic church as a child. Growing up, I attended church sporadically. We both had a belief and faith in God as adults but still had much to learn about him and what role his word plays in our lives. Memorized scriptures are meaningless without living as a testament to his power. When Matthew was born, I don't think either of us were in a place yet where we fully understood the importance and significance of Christ. But Matthew was the teacher who showed us what all of it meant. Even as an infant, that sense of God's light surrounding him was ever present. We later came to understand why this was.

As he grew, we grew as parents and as people. Babies don't come with instructions, so parents learn by trial and error. We worked into a parenting style that was comfortable for us. For the most part we agreed with each other's ideas and approaches. Parenting Matthew was uncomplicated because he was always so easygoing. We could tell him something once and that was it. He detested getting into trouble, so he would go out of his way to ensure that he didn't do anything that would disappoint us. "Pleaser" is the one word that can be used to describe him, always hoping to delight.

Our family dynamics changed and evolved exponentially the first few years of Matthew's life. We had career changes, a move—and the birth of our second child. In May 2004, we received the news we had again prayed for. Our family would soon be a family of four. Our life felt so full up to this point, yet we knew an element was missing: a sibling for Matthew. Matthew was about to turn two, and we felt that the spacing was good to have another baby. Matthew was ecstatic at the idea of having a sibling. He never thought of it in the way that our family was gaining a new member. It was always "his baby."

My pregnancy proved to be yet another test of physical and emotional strength. But as we had always done, Billy and I turned to our belief that Christ holds the plans for our futures. The excitement of these new changes in our lives brought great pleasure. As we trusted in the words we lifted to the heavens, we felt God giving us the continued assurance that He had it all under control.

At sixteen weeks we found out that we were having another boy. We were elated, and Matthew was so excited to have a little brother. His name was chosen, and Conner Charles was due in January 2005. Just as with Matthew, contractions came much earlier than expected, this time at around twenty-seven weeks. I was put on complete bed rest and required a couple of hospitalizations to keep him from being delivered early. Finally, after thirty-five weeks of pregnancy, our next little angel joined our family. On December 14, 2004, at 5:25 p.m., Conner Charles Goodwin was born.

This time we weren't as lucky to keep a newborn out of the NICU. He required a couple of days in intensive care due to breathing complications. Little did we know at the time, but this was kind of a starter course for us when it comes to hospitals.

Matthew had his little brother at last. Now we felt complete as a family—three had become four.

five

AND THE RAIN STARTS

In the four years since Matthew's birth, life had continued with all of the ups and downs most families face. We continued on one day at a time with dreams and goals as a family. As Matthew grew, Billy and I often discussed what our educational choices would be for our children. One of the most important aspects to us as Christians was for our children to openly pray in school and give thanks to God. We have always taught our children that they can turn to God for anything and should seek his guidance in every aspect of their lives. We also wanted our children to be academically challenged to their fullest potential. As a mother I needed to know that my children would be nurtured at school in ways they would at home. We found all of the ingredients at Parkview Baptist Preschool.

I looked forward to Matthew starting preschool for the first time in the fall of 2006. When we got a call in the summer saying that Matthew had been accepted to Parkview Baptist Preschool, we were thrilled. The thought of Matthew making new friends was exciting, and we would grow to love the faculty and staff as family. When God placed us at Parkview, we couldn't have had any idea how important this school family would become to us in later months as tragic events unfolded.

That first September morning, Conner and I walked Matthew to his class. Inside, I wanted to melt, but I put on a brave face for him. After all, I was bringing him to half-day preschool, not dropping him off to become a foreign exchange student for a year. Miss Connie eagerly met him and assured me he would be okay. I had no idea at that first meeting the impact she would have in my life. I looked around at the other kids and panicked at the thought of him not making friends. A little boy walked over and immediately wanted to play. Conner and I exchanged kisses and hugs with Matthew, and we made it out the door. Just in time! Here came the tears. The two of us cried the entire way through the parking lot and sat for nearly twenty minutes sobbing inside the car. How slowly can the hands on a clock move when you are ready for it to be a certain time? One o'clock wasn't coming quick enough. He was all smiles when I finally got him. The first day was a success! "I can do it again tomorrow," he said, and I just thought, *That's just great, but I don't know if Mom can.*

The schedule became comfortable, and Conner adjusted to not having his big brother home with him. Our new daily routines felt natural. As late fall etched closer, the preschool activities got into full gear. I was amazed at how much he was learning academically, emotionally, and spiritually. We watched his love for God grow and saw him relish in the teachings during Bible lessons. As he learned the basics of the alphabet and numbers, he also developed a deeper love of scripture. This love coupled with the teachings of his sporadic Sunday school classes planted his desire to learn everything he possibly could about the Bible. Even today he amazes us with his knowledge of the Old Testament and the depth of his understanding of key figures in the body of Christianity.

When school started Matthew jumped in with both feet. We were so proud of him and how much he was learning. My life had finally reached the point that I had always dreamed of. I had absolutely everything I could possibly want emotionally. I felt so remarkably blessed to have so much. God had given me an awesome husband, two amazing little boys, a new home right next door to my parents, a wonderful family, and a new business. This was it. I could turn cruise control on now.

November was approaching, and Matthew was so excited about his Thanksgiving party at school. His room mothers had so many cool things planned for them to do, and he couldn't wait to show it all off. The day of his party finally arrived. I was excited because this was the last day of school before the week of Thanksgiving holidays. But, oddly, Matthew wasn't perky that morning, or at least not as perky as he should have been considering it was party day. Luckily, everything went great. They wore their feather headbands they made, and they shucked corn. All of the little ones sang the songs they had been working so hard to learn. I was so proud! By that afternoon, he was worn out. I assumed we were getting yet another "bug." Although he never really got sick enough for a trip to the doctor, he just felt weak and didn't have much energy. He took it easy and enjoyed the week off.

By the time school started again the week after Thanksgiving, everyone was already looking forward to Christmas. What an exciting time as we celebrate the birth of Our Lord and Savior! This year would be extra special because it would start the tradition I had been waiting for: the homemade ornaments from school that I knew would adorn the tree for years to come. During all of the festivities it was constantly instilled into the children the true meaning of Christmas.

In the midst of pre-holiday projects, I got a call one day from school to say that Matthew wasn't feeling well and that I should come pick him up. He was in the office with a garbage can in front of him when I arrived, saying he felt like he was going to throw up. He was really warm, so I decided to take him in to the doctor. He was diagnosed with strep throat and an ear infection. Ten days of antibiotics and all should be fine. Matthew never once protested against taking his medicines. He knew he needed them and wanted to feel better, and he had improved by the end of the ten days and was looking forward to his class's Christmas party.

The Christmas party was more of an experience than a party. The celebration of the birth of Jesus is always a great celebration at Parkview, and this year was no different. The children had been working with the room mothers and their teacher, Miss Connie, to make the ornaments to remember this sacred holiday. I couldn't wait to get Matthew's on the tree when we got home. After the party, everyone said their good-byes, and wished a "Merry Christmas."

A few days before Christmas, during the break, Matthew grew sick again. This time he suffered with a high fever, dark circles under his eyes, and nausea. Once again, the diagnosis was strep throat and double ear infection. And again, he started the antibiotics to clear it all up. It was decided that we would take it easy that year for Christmas and New Year's. The traditional Christmas Eve barbecue was to take place, but we would just be eating inside this year. Both boys were tucked in after dinner, and they excitedly went to sleep to await Santa's arrival Christmas morning. Matthew went to bed still not feeling well.

At around 1:00 a.m., Matthew woke up and came into our room. He did his best to convince us it was time to get up and open presents. As every parent does in this situation, we rationalized with him that Santa may not have come yet, and his brother was not yet up. We had to wait until at least daylight, but his insistence continued. Within a few minutes he reached near hysteria, and his behavior caught our attention. Matthew has never been one of those children to have breakdowns over the slightest things. We found his demanding, irrational behavior to be out of character. Then Conner came down the hall. Now the whole family was awake. We were pleading with Matthew to go back to sleep for a little while longer.

After over an hour of pleading, we weren't getting anywhere. Off we went to the living room to see if Santa had come to our home. Yes, and he had left presents. After the presents were opened and the paper was scattered, the boys decided it would now be okay to go lie back down. They crawled into bed with Billy and me and went back to sleep. I remember wrapping my arm around Matthew and feeling his little heart beat so rapidly. Matthew had plenty of time to calm down since the hysterics a few hours earlier, but I assumed that everything was okay. If there was anything to be concerned about, surely something would have been caught at one of his doctor's appointments.

Over the next couple of months, a pattern developed of constant ear infections, strep throat, and viruses. As soon as one course of antibiotics was completed, we were onto to the next round within a few weeks. Finally, his pediatrician said it was time to discuss seeing an ENT for tubes to be placed in his ears. His ears weren't draining, which caused the recurrent infections. We scheduled the appointment, and the ENT agreed with his pediatrician that he did indeed need tubes placed in his ears. He also had enlarged adenoids, and they and his tonsils needed to be removed. Removing his adenoids, the doctors told us, could make a difference in his weak appetite and sleeping patterns as well. Matthew had never been a big eater, and we hoped his appetite would pick up. The doctors assured us the procedures could all be done at once. I prayed that those procedures would be the answer to help Matthew finally feel better.

six

A FATHER'S INTUITION

B illy and I were apprehensive about Matthew's surgery. We didn't like the idea of our little one having this procedure but realized that it could be the best thing for him, given how often he had been sick the past couple of months. However, I felt more than just anxiety or nerves over an unknown situation. It was almost a feeling of dread. As much as we tried to tell ourselves that this had to be done so the infections would stop, the distressing feeling just wouldn't go away.

Billy was especially anguished about the entire process. The apprehension almost consumed him. From the moment I called him after leaving the ENT's office, he repeated over and over, "Celeste, I just don't feel good about this." When I would ask him what gave him that feeling, he said it was a gut instinct. He didn't believe it would be as simple as the doctors said it would be. When anything was mentioned about the upcoming surgery, Billy would get a look of immediate concern. He carried a sense of trepidation for the days leading up to the actual surgery. I kept assuring him that it was a routine procedure done on thousands of kids every day, but Billy's only solace was faith in God and his love for Matthew. Billy has always been a father who errs on the side of caution when it comes to his two children, sometimes even going a bit overboard with certain situations. When we first brought Matthew home as a newborn, Billy tried to make sure everything was perfect for his new son and help out while I recovered from my cesarean section. One night I heard Billy and my sister, Doretta, in the kitchen and could smell a foul odor. I slowly got up and found them attempting to boil the plastic disposable bottles we were given at the hospital. Looking back now, it is quite funny. At the time, he just wanted to make sure everything was ideal. His cautious nature was no different when it came to Matthew's upcoming surgery. But the magnitude of his concern was so much greater and intense.

I tried to calm Billy's worries about the surgery, but he repeated over and over that this was the beginning of something terrible. What that "terrible" was couldn't be described with words. An overpowering feeling of worry was ever present.

A couple of days before the surgery we sat down and questioned any alternative to the procedure. We didn't find any. The surgery was truly necessary in order for the multitude of infections to finally cease. We realized that taking round after round of antibiotics was not good for Matthew either. The possibility of Matthew's body becoming resistant to some medications if taken for too long was always there, and his immune system also would be weakened.

After extreme hesitation and much prayer, we scheduled the surgery for March 28, 2007. I was given all of our pre-operative instructions. Billy found it difficult to even look over the parent copy of the paperwork that we brought home. No aspirin products for two weeks prior and nothing to eat or drink after midnight the day of surgery. Matthew also needed a pre-op visit with his pediatrician for a check-up and to get the proper paperwork filled out for the surgery center. His height and weight were measured, plus his temperature and his blood pressure were also taken. Blood pressure? That was different. I couldn't remember whether Matthew had ever had a blood pressure reading before. Being naïve, I assumed it was a necessary part of the process. I wasn't sure what the significance of this measurement was. I made sure I had all of the paperwork and got it back to the ENT's office. We were all set.

The afternoon before surgery, Matthew was given a choice of restaurants for dinner. It would be quite a few days before he would be back to a normal diet. Even though we enjoyed a great dinner at Outback and giggled with the boys, I could see the concern and anxiety on Billy's face. Afterward we headed back home to get ready for the next morning. I went over the checklist and made sure we had everything we needed. It was only an outpatient procedure, and we were to be home by late morning, so not a whole lot that needed to be packed. Plans were made for eating Jell-O and Popsicles the next day, along with some lounging around. As we went to bed that night, we prayed for God to be with Matthew the next day so he wouldn't be scared. I think Mommy and Daddy may have needed those prayers more than he did.

Because we had to leave so early, Conner spent the night before surgery with my mom, so he could sleep in the next morning. A welcome sleepover at Maw Maw's was just fine for him. We didn't pack a bag; he was just going to be next door for one night. Our plans were to pick him up when we returned home from the surgery center.

If I could turn back the hands of time, I would have done a lot of things differently that night. I would have kissed Conner for the fourth time, instead of just stopping at three. Sometimes it's at their request, but mostly I go back for just one more for me. I knew they would be too big for that one day, and I tried to get as many in as I could. It would be many nights before I got to tuck him in again.

Traffic was light on the drive to Baton Rouge that morning. The sun was still not up when we arrived at the surgery center. I would come to know quite vividly how night turns to morning over the next few weeks. Before Matthew was taken into the operating room, we sat in a pre-op area to answer some standard medical history questions. We gave the nurse all of the pre-op physical information from his pediatrician she requested while she took his vitals.

After his last vital, the nurse called for the anesthesiologist to come and meet with us. The doctor had looked over the paperwork that the nurse gave to him and went over a few other questions with us. He then asked her to take the blood pressure again. There was almost a questionable pause on the anesthesiologist's face. I so wish I could have had some insight into what his hesitation meant for my child and his safety and well-being. After a moment he told us it would be just a little while, and then they would get started. And very shortly, Matthew was taken to the operating room.

Billy and I nervously waited for word that the surgery was completed. The procedure was routine, and I kept trying to reassure Billy and myself that everything would be just fine. I knew the anxiety would lift as soon as we could see and hold Matthew again. In the waiting area were families of children who went into surgery after Matthew, but their children were being sent to recovery before Matthew. After this happened a couple of times, we justified that maybe those children had different procedures done and therefore, they may not have needed as much time in the operating room. Still, it was unsettling each time we hear someone else's name be called.

When our name was finally called, it was by a nurse from another area. She motioned for us to follow. As we walked down the hall, she explained that we would be meeting the doctor in a consultation room to discuss how the procedure went. In a few minutes, the door opened and in walked the doctor who had performed the surgery. With a very matter-of-fact tone, he advised us that the surgery went perfectly. There had been no complications. The doctor successfully placed tubes in each ear and removed Matthew's tonsils and adenoids. What a relief! *Thank you, God, for hearing our prayers to keep him safe.* Other than the facts that had been presented to us, not a word of any other issue was mentioned. We were told he was on his way to recovery, and we could join him as soon as the nurses were ready.

With a sigh of relief, we returned to the waiting area in anticipation of seeing Matthew in recovery. This was welcome news and I hoped it would put to rest any remaining anxieties Billy had about this entire ordeal. As we sat down, I asked Billy, "Do you feel better now?"

With the deepest look on his face, he said, "No, I really don't. Celeste, something is still telling me that he is not okay."

I couldn't understand why this nagging feeling was persisting. We sat in silence for the remaining minutes before we were allowed into recovery. I paused and silently sent up a prayer, *God, thank you for protecting Matthew. Father, I ask that you place peace and understanding on Billy to know that Matthew is okay.*

Finally, we heard what we had been waiting for. The nurse called for the parents of Matthew Goodwin. We were led to his bed. He was still very groggy and was not feeling well. We learned that day that waking up from anesthesia is not one of the easiest things for Matthew to do. I was allowed to rock him and give him time to wake fully. His recovery nurse returned frequently to monitor his blood pressure and temperature. After a couple of hours, we were told he was fine to go home. Again we were told that everything went fine during surgery and recovery. There was absolutely no indication that we had anything to worry about. We believed he would be back to normal in just a few days.

When we were finally given approval to leave, it was a relief. The fears that Billy had held in his mind seemed as though they were all for nothing, just an overly worried parent's fears about a minor procedure. This feeling of reprieve would be short lived, though. Matthew was insistent on seeing his Maw Maw and Ghe Ghe when we got home, so Billy pulled into their driveway, and I carried Matthew inside. We needed to pick up Conner as well. My mom already had the typical tonsillectomy goodies—ice cream—ready for when he felt up to them. Within an hour of being home, Matthew wanted to eat grits. Grits! That was awesome. He must have been feeling super great, and he did manage to eat about half a bowl. We gathered Conner up, headed out the back door, and walked across the yard to our house. Matthew lay down on the couch in his pajamas to take a nap.

I curled up in the recliner and thought, *Well, that wasn't so bad after all. I guess it could have been worse. He should be on the mend really soon.* Matthew woke up from his nap feeling a little uncomfortable as to be expected, but otherwise okay. The doctor sent us home with a prescription for Lortab. Around 4:00 p.m., he took the dose and was waiting for Nanny Dawn to stop for a visit on her way home.

Nanny Dawn arrived with more goodies: mini ice cream packs, a card, and a balloon. While they were visiting I noticed something strange. Matthew's cheeks had started to swell and looked unusual. Immediately I called the ENT service to find out what to do. The on-call physician suggested that I give him a dose of over-the-counter Benadryl to counteract the swelling. This could have been a reaction to the Lortab that he took earlier. As instructed, I gave him the appropriate dosage for his height and weight. Typically Benadryl will make people sleepy, so I expected that he would probably want to go back to bed. He finished his visit with Nanny Dawn and lay back down on the couch.

Within just a few minutes, he started complaining of not feeling well but couldn't completely describe what was wrong. He said he just felt really bad, and his stomach was upset. After I explained to him about the fact that he would probably feel bad off and on for the next couple of days, he said he thought he was going to throw up. He ran into the bathroom and began to vomit. This was the first vomiting episode that would end up lasting six days straight. He was vomiting blood. Initially, it was brown and appeared to be old blood that may have settled in his stomach during surgery. But by the second round of throwing up, it was bright red. I knew that this meant new blood, and he had to be bleeding somewhere. Eventually we calmed him down enough to lie down, so we could take a look in his mouth. Billy proceeded to look in his throat and saw that one of the incisions appeared to be open. It must have popped open from the vomiting.

I again called the ENT service to tell them of this new issue. The advice of the doctor was to bring him in to the emergency room to check the extent of the open incision and the bleeding and also to make sure that he stopped throwing up and didn't dehydrate. Sometimes people can have an adverse reaction to anesthesia, and this can cause them to vomit several hours following surgery. Matthew was upset and wanted my mom to go with us to the emergency room. We left Billy at home to take care of Conner until we returned. By 5:00 p.m. we were on our way back to Baton Rouge. I assumed we would wait an hour or two, be seen by a doctor, be given some medicine, and be back at home by midnight or so. The arrival and wait at the emergency room was uneventful. Matthew continued to throw up, and finally we were in an exam room and waiting for a doctor. After his examination the doctor determined that part of the incision in his throat had opened slightly, and this is probably where the blood came from. But by this time, it already looked better, and he was not vomiting blood when he threw up. The initial diagnosis was that a reaction to the anesthesia had caused the stomach upset. The main concern was dehydration if the vomiting didn't stop.

By now, it was around 9:00 p.m., and time for his next dose of pain medicine. After explaining the earlier reaction to Lortab with swelling, it was decided that this time to give him morphine to control his pain. Within ten minutes of receiving this medication, Matthew began to have facial swelling again, plus some difficulty breathing. Only this time, it was worse than before. Once again we used Benadryl to counteract the reaction.

Between a break in the vomiting episodes, his ER doctor came in briefly to say she felt that the anti-nausea medicine was working and he was okay to go home. She left the room to write his discharge papers, and my mom and I looked at each other with relief. This was around 10:00 p.m. or so. As initially planned, we could be home by midnight and crawl into bed. Matthew had even been able to eat a popsicle and hold it down for nearly thirty minutes. We believed we were in the clear!

No such luck. Matthew repositioned himself in bed and once again, here came the vomit. I opened the door to let the doctor know. She came back in and said that unfortunately she would not be able to send him home because he could dehydrate. We were advised it would be best to simply put him in a room overnight on some IV fluids, and he would be okay to go home in the morning. It was not great news but not horrible news, either. It would be better for Matthew to make sure he had plenty of fluids. The doctor was reassuring that this type of thing happens all the time after anesthesia. Fortunately, it should be out of his system in a few hours, and all would be fine. Knowing that Billy typically becomes nauseated from anesthesia assured me that this must also be the case for Matthew.

I called Billy to update him and make sure he didn't worry. He understood, having experienced this himself before. The next call went to my sister to ask her to come pick up our mom from the hospital. She would need to be home first thing in the morning to watch Conner, so Billy could get to work. With all the arrangements made, we waited patiently for a room to open upstairs on the pediatric floor, which could take a long time. Later, a nurse started his IV. Before this morning he had never had an IV. I watched as four veins were blown while she tried to thread the needle in. We didn't know it at the time, but Matthew's blood pressure was so high, the elevated pressure made it difficult to start an IV. No parent wants to watch her baby get a shot or have a needle put in. But to watch it four times? All the while, Matthew continued to throw up.

After several hours of waiting, a room was finally ready and Matthew could get into a comfortable bed and rest. A nurse wheeled in a wheelchair, but he refused to get in unless I sat in it and he rode on my lap. Off we went upstairs. Ah, the room was so much more comfortable than the emergency room. It was not a four-star hotel by any means, but an improvement over the past few hours. By this time, it was 1:00 a.m., hours since we arrived at the hospital—not exactly speedy. A sweet nurse came in and introduced herself to say she would be taking care of Matthew that night. I thought, *Well, most of the night is gone and we'll be out of here by early morning. This throwing up stuff should be stopping any minute.* She asked if we have ever been to the hospital before. I told her this was the first and hopefully last time. She explained that she would check his vitals every four hours, and if we needed anything to let her know. He was only there for observation and fluids. That sounded easy enough. She returned a while later with all the necessary equipment to do her job.

At this point, Matthew's blood pressure was taken—something

that had not happened once since our initial arrival in the emergency room. The last time it was taken was the day before at the surgery center before we were discharged to go home. A puzzled look appeared on her face, and she kind of gave the blood pressure machine a questionable stare.

She said, "I'll be right back." She wheeled the machine out and came back with a different machine. "Let's try this again," she said. She placed the cuff on his arm and it began to inflate. A confused look appeared again on her face. Her words were, "That can't be right." She left the room yet again and returned with a third machine. I thought flippantly, *You would certainly expect such a big hospital to have working equipment.*

I was not worried at this point because after all, their machines were malfunctioning. After the third machine, she left and returned with backup. One of the nursing supervisors came in to see what was going on. The cuff was placed on his arm and the reading was calculated. The reading was 195 systolic over 135 diastolic. Alarmed, the nursing supervisor explained that this was an extremely high reading for a child of his size and age. She needed to call the doctor immediately and see what he would advise them to do. She returned to say that after consulting with both the ER doctor and the on-call ENT, they suggested watching him for the next few hours and see if the pressure went down. They thought the anesthesia from surgery the day before was the culprit. They expected Matthew's blood pressure would go down on its own in a couple of hour's time. A precautionary call was also made to the on-call PICU physician to notify them of the situation and let them know he was being monitored closely.

I was not a medically-savvy person at that point in my life, and I kind of liked it that way. I knew when to get worried about a fever and how to put a Band-Aid on a cut. After that, it was over my head. I did not know what high blood pressure was or that it could happen to a small child. In my naïve mind, I assumed that as people aged, their blood pressure could go up, But, with diet and medicine, it could be controlled. I had no idea it could be so serious or even deadly. Things have changed since then, and my education in medical terminology and conditions has grown considerably. Not by choice, but out of necessity.

To put it into perspective, a normal four-year-old male should have a systolic reading around 90 and a diastolic reading around 60. Matthew's pressure was 195/135, which was definitely out of the acceptable limits. I still get chills on my neck when I think about that first reading. I think my naïveté worked in my favor that night. I didn't panic.

During the next few hours he continued to throw up but never really complained of anything else. Other than the vomiting, one probably would not have thought there was anything seriously wrong. He was not crying or complaining. I called Billy around 6:00 a.m. to make sure he got Conner to my mom's and to let him know that I planned to be home in a couple of hours. I explained that Matthew and I would spend the day catching up on some much-needed sleep. I told Billy of the initial finding of a high blood pressure, but everyone guessed it was probably from the anesthesia. A little while later, I went to the restroom, and the nurse came in to do vitals.

I assumed all was well, or else someone would have said something. The "something" came in the form of a PICU intensivist physician sitting on the foot of Matthew's bed explaining to me that a high blood pressure reading in a child of Matthew's age was a very serious issue. It was still slightly possible that it could be from anesthesia. He wanted me to know that the intensive care physicians had been notified of Matthew's readings and condition and were monitoring him carefully. Thirty minutes later another reading was taken, and this time yet another PICU physician visited our room. She was calm but serious and matter-of-fact in her information. She spoke with urgency to put into perspective the seriousness of Matthew's condition. As she talked, my stomach tightened and I felt flushed. My hands immediately began to shake and I was absolutely scared.

What was happening? It was impossible to wrap my head around the words that kept coming from these medical professionals. The surgery was supposed to be simple. We were told that it went fine the day before and nothing was out of the ordinary. But now we were on the brink of Matthew being admitted to the pediatric intensive care unit.

I was told that some of the causes of Matthew's high blood pressure, which was clearly not anesthesia related ay this point, could be brain tumor, heart defect, renal (kidney) tumors, or other cardiology and renal issues. All of the conditions were extremely serious and possibly even life-threatening. She calmly explained to me that Matthew would immediately be transferred to the PICU for further evaluation and testing. After she left, I sat with a stunned look on my face and thought, *What just happened?*

seven

INTRODUCTION
TO THE PICU

S till stunned, I picked up the phone and dialed Billy's cell phone number.

"Matthew is being transferred to the PICU!" I blurted out.

He was already at work across the Mississippi River in Donaldsonville by this time. After all, I did tell him that we would probably be home before lunch.

"What are you talking about?" he quickly asked, worried. "What's wrong?" I explained what had transpired over the past forty-five minutes and told him that Matthew wasn't any better and his condition had worsened. But I told him that he needed to get back to Baton Rouge as soon as possible, which was at least a forty-five minute drive. He assured me that he would head to Baton Rouge as soon as he could. All of his nightmarish feelings of the past weeks were coming to fruition. How right he had been about the minor procedure being the beginning of something terrible.

Immediately after speaking to him, I had to call my mom. Conner was with her, and she needed to know that the stay was indefinite at this point. I explained the situation and told her that I needed my sister, Doretta, to bring me a change of clothes. Doretta was getting ready for work and she called her boss to explain there was a family emergency.

The third call went to Matthew's godmother, Dawn. Dawn and I have been friends for over a decade. When Matthew was born she was in the operating room with me and wiped the tears out of my eyes the first time I heard him cry. She also happened to be a registered nurse at the same hospital where Matthew was now a patient. I told her what was happening and, like always, she was there as soon as I needed her. I have been blessed with some really great friends in my life. Dawn is truly one of those.

Aunt Retta and Nanny Dawn sat with Matthew while I ran into the bathroom to change clothes and brush my teeth before we made the trek to the PICU. I didn't know what to expect; I was nervous about my baby needing such intensive care. *What could be wrong? Why is this happening to him? He's only four.* With my hand on the bathroom doorknob, I pleaded with God to make all of this a bad dream. I emerged reluctantly. If I knew it would make the terror all go away, I would have sat in that bathroom forever.

Nothing in our four years of parenting prepared us for how to deal with the trials that would come the moment I walked through the double doors from the pediatric floor into the pediatric intensive care unit. My stomach knotted, and I didn't know if I would throw up or pass out. The look on Matthew's face was sheer terror, and he finally got upset. Prior to that moment, he had been relatively calm. The parenting books don't have a chapter addressing how to explain to your child what a PICU is and why he is going there.

Sheer panic set in for me. The first bed that I saw had the tiniest little person in it. Matthew looked like an ant at the bottom of a skyscraper under all of the tubes and wires that were keeping him alive. Yet, I could see that he had the most beautiful little face despite all the equipment around him. Never had I seen something so intense. People stood around him, crying and praying. I began having dreadful thoughts, wondering why they were crying and praying. It felt like something on TV, and not my real life.

We passed several rooms, which were more like cubbies with curtains. The nurses' station was one long desk, the entire length of the floor, and it was directly across from Matthew's room. Abuzz with activity 24/7, the doctors, nurses, and other personnel came and went. Matthew was put on the bed and was crying nervously. The nursing supervisor was getting him settled so that all of his monitors and leads could be hooked up and his plan of care could be established and put into motion. Once he was settled, Doretta had to run to work. She didn't want to leave, but I assured her we didn't need anything and it would be fine. This was really more reassurance for myself than for her. Billy would be there soon.

Within minutes, the doctors whom I had met earlier in the morning were again with me, going over questions as they put the pieces together to figure out why my son was so sick. An arterial line had to be immediately placed into an artery to give continuous blood pressure readings. It would be painful to have put in, and Matthew needed to be sedated in order to do so. It would be a bedside procedure, so the medicine to sedate would go directly into his IV. I had seen the IV being placed, and even though it was unpleasant and hurt him, it was over pretty quickly.

During the frenzied commotion of admitting a child into the PICU, Matthew calmed down. You could see the fear in his eyes, but he never complained. In a brief pause between nurses and doctors, he looked up at me and said, "Mommy, please don't leave me by myself."

I fought back tears and replied, "Matthew, I'll be right here. I can't leave you because I love you." I gave him a quick smile and said, "You can't leave me either, okay?"

Just in the past few hours, I could see that Matthew's condition was rapidly declining. The severity of what was plaguing him was powerful. For the first time, I sensed that Matthew's life was truly in danger. An intense emotion rolled over me like a dump truck. This little boy was only four years old and his entire life lay before him. I pleaded with God, *Please see that Matthew has a great purpose and heal his body.*

In what seemed like a few seconds, two PICU physicians, and five nurses stood with me around the bed. They quickly flocked in like birds. As the doctors talked to me, the work began. The medication to sedate him was administered, and he quickly fell asleep. Because he had just had a tonsillectomy, he could not be intubated. Therefore, one of the doctors, stood at his head and manually kept his airway open making sure he was breathing okay. The other physician worked on placing the arterial line. I truly wish someone told me to get out of there. Never, and I mean *never*, do I want to see that kind of pain inflicted upon one of my children again. Words aren't strong enough to convey what took place over the next twenty minutes.

The intensity in the air was so profound. Matthew fell asleep, but even through the sedation he felt every single probe into his artery. His little body jerked with each push of the probe. It was not an easy placement. His systolic blood pressure was nearing 200, and the blood pulsated through his veins. With each beat of his heart, it would pump the blood faster, which would push the arterial line out with the pulses. They tried the right wrist first and made unsuccessful sticks. Then, they moved on to the left wrist. Again, no luck on that side.

Billy finally arrived at the hospital during this frantic chaos. The panic on his face was indescribable. I couldn't say anything. The words wouldn't come out. He stood beside me for a minute, but then we walked out of the unit. Billy's parents were outside; they had driven him to Baton Rouge. I don't think he could have made the drive by himself safely because he was really shaken up. When we walked through the doors, I broke down. No longer could I keep my emotions in check. I guess I held it until I saw Billy. I knew that I needed him to be with me before I could let go.

My body physically ached at how deeply I was hurting for my son. Why had God allowed this to happen? Matthew was an innocent child and twenty-four hours earlier was seemingly healthy besides some ear infections. I tried to explain through the sobs what little information had been obtained from the doctors and the possible causes for this crisis. As each possibility came out of my mouth, the reality of what they each were set in. The situation became real at this point. Our child had something more than a simple ear infection. He had more than the common cold. He was in the PICU on the verge of coma, stroke, or even worse. All the while, his little body was being afflicted with pain in the name of medicine to place the arterial line.

We took a few minutes to collect ourselves as best we could before walking back into the unit. When we returned, the doctors told us a battery of tests were needed immediately. At first, I prayed for all of the things that I didn't want them to find. As each test came back negative for this disease and that condition, I prayed for them to just find something, find what was causing my child to be so sick so we could fix it and move on. I continually asked God to give us answers. I wanted answers because with them came solutions.

I received another crash course in patience that day. Patience is not something that has come easily to me my entire life. I want to see results instantly. No matter what I am searching for, I just hate to wait. Billy and I both learned that we needed to listen carefully to what was being said to us and by whom. We learned that time is the enemy when you have a sick baby, time that you feel is being wasted while your child was unable to run and play like other children.

eight

THE ROCKS

Pure horror evolved as thoughts of what had happened to our son and our world in the past twenty-four hours swirled around. How had our seemingly healthy, vibrant son turned into a frail little body fighting for another day? I could hardly comprehend it. The next few days were the most scary, terrifying, and uncertain time of our lives. Our families and friends immediately set up prayer chains asking anyone and everyone they knew to send prayers for Matthew. Hopelessness was beginning to seep into every hour that passed without finding a cause. We held vigil hour after hour, slowly watching our child slip further and further away. We prayed for the vomiting to stop and the blood pressure to decrease. We prayed for an answer to why all of this had happened and for the healing of his body and spirit.

The test of people's character comes at times of crisis. You find out where your rocks are, where your support is. I can look back and say that my heart is full when I think of just how many rocks we had during that time. We were supported by calls and messages from

Celeste and Grandma Massey, 1975

so many who were praying for him. We were sustained by so many prayer warriors. I continued to ask vigilantly for healing for my baby. Many times I would ask in my own prayers for God to allow his angels, those whom I loved dearly who had passed, to protect Matthew and give him comfort.

One of the angels I asked for in particular was my Grandma Massey. She was always a protector. Since her passing when I was fourteen, I often asked for God to allow her to help me in difficult times. More often than not, I felt her presence with me when I needed it. This event in my life would once again give evidence to the fact that angels are, indeed, there to guard those who need it most. My grandmother would soon be giving Matthew the same comfort she provided to me so many years before he was even born. But this time Matthew would testify of the beauty that awaits us all where the angels dwell.

From the moment Matthew was admitted, I set up bedside vigil. I refused to leave his side until Billy would force me to just take a walk to clear my head for a few minutes. I couldn't eat, didn't sleep, and felt helpless. I called Matthew's other godmother, Melissa, while he was having his CT done and told her of the events that had unfolded. Melissa immediately left work and rushed to be with us. She prayed with us, cried with us, and gave reassurance it was all in God's hands and he would protect Matthew. I wanted to believe that with every fiber of my being. All we could do was pray.

That first evening was torture and unimaginably long. Doretta came back to the hospital after work, and she, along with Billy's parents, Mr. Bill and Miss Carol, sat with us while we waited to hear results. All we kept getting back were negative tests and inconclusive answers. Billy and I discussed briefly how we would just take things hour by hour and adjust accordingly. We had no way to make a plan because we just didn't know what tomorrow would hold.

Billy's brother, Ryan, and his wife, Supriya, had been in constant contact all day from Houston. Billy needed and welcomed the comfort of his brother. His world was upside down, and he was a nervous wreck. Uncle Kurt and Aunt Mandy, Matthew's uncle and aunt came as soon as they could. Before bringing Mandy into the unit, I briefly updated her on Matthew's condition and what to expect when we went in. It was hard to prepare people to see Matthew when the last time everyone saw him he was just a typical little boy. Mandy's eyes filled with tears as soon as she saw him. His body was weak, and tubes, lines, and monitors were running everywhere. She kept telling him how much he was loved and that God would protect him.

We decided that I would stay the night with Matthew, and Billy would return in the morning. Billy went home to check on Conner and get a few hours of rest. It is hard for people to understand the level of trauma it causes to a sibling who has to endure having a brother or sister that is critically or chronically ill. Siblings are often forgotten in the day-to-day seriousness of the disease. But they are an integral part of a family, and their hearts hurt just like everyone else's. They may show it differently because they are young, but the emotion is still there. From the beginning we tried to keep Conner as stable and included as we could for his age level.

During that night we learned that a hospital never shuts down. It is a twenty-four-hour continuous caravan of people and departments doing what is necessary to get people well. The team of doctors Matthew had in the PICU were unparalleled. They spoke to me in clear, understandable terms. They were open in what they knew and what they didn't. We were visited every couple of hours by one of the physicians as they evaluated and checked his status continually. The doctors' frustration was apparent after each test offered no clear answer.

That night was spent with an endless cycle of vomiting and a steady decline. Matthew did not sleep, did not cry, and did not speak. He just lay there. He would motion to me when he knew he would throw up and then lay back down just as quiet and easy. His color was sickly pale. His eyes were sunk in, and he developed huge black circles around them. He did not eat, so he lost weight rapidly. I so badly wanted an answer so we could turn this progression around. He was literally dying a little more each day right in front of my eyes.

Billy was at the hospital before five the next morning. I refused to leave. The second day was much like the first. As the second evening rolled around, Billy again went home at my urging to check on Conner. I was physically exhausted but could not leave my son. Billy wanted to stay, but he knew Conner needed him too. Matthew had now been vomiting continuously since arriving. Other medications were tried in combination with the Benadryl to stop the vomiting but to no avail. Out of desperation I called Matthew's uncle Kyle around 10:00 p.m. to come help me for a few hours. He spent that night with Matthew and me, taking good care of him. Kyle realized that Matthew's monitors clearly indicated when Matthew was going to vomit. We could see his heart rate and blood pressure increase rather rapidly, and then we knew that he was about to throw up. Kyle sat in a chair all night and watched the monitors. When he saw the numbers getting higher, he would get the bucket and cool towel ready. I don't know if he knows how much I appreciate what he did that night.

nine

WHICH WAY TO GO

The next several days were an endless hamster wheel of medications, tests, and long waits. Matthew continued to slip further and further away from us without any answers. Sounds and activity affected him and became life threatening because his blood pressure would elevate dangerously high with the slightest stimulation. Matthew was acutely aware of everything that was going on around him. His monitors would show just how much he was impacted by stimulation, and his blood pressure and heart rate would rise quickly.

I know that God places people in our lives for specific reasons. God has laid in our path some truly amazing people. One of those was an amazing PICU nurse named Kristi. She was a straight to the point, caring woman who seemed to have an affection for Matthew and his struggles. During her first shift of caring for Matthew, she realized how he was being affected by different stimulation. She went above and beyond what is necessary and made arrangements to have Matthew moved further down in the unit to one of the more quiet and private PICU rooms. This room actually had a door that could be closed. I was grateful because it also had a bathroom. No more running down the hall for me. Matthew had become so weak that he was confined to the bed and had to use the urinal when he needed to go to the restroom. Kristi took her job to heart and made a lasting impression on us that we still feel to this day. Years later I had the opportunity to publicly thank her for her kindness and care during a workshop where we reconnected.

After getting into the quieter room, Matthew lay in a dark environment. We still had no answers about why all of this was happening. His nurses posted a sign on the door that visitors were limited and could only stay for a few minutes. Matthew has always been one who feels like he needs to be social and pleasant all the time. Under normal circumstances, every parent wants that for his child. However, the time wasn't right for him to make others feel welcomed. Thankfully, all of our family and friends understood that this was for his protection and well-being.

We were inundated with constant rounds by the doctors and nurses. They were either checking his status, giving meds, or informing us of where they were in his care. One night in particular, around 2:00 a.m., one of his doctors came into his room, kneeled down under his monitor with coffee cup in hand, and stared at the monitor for the longest time. He said nothing, just looked and pondered.

Finally, after a long silence, he turned to me and said, "Mrs. Goodwin, I just don't have an answer for you. And it is killing me that I can't tell you what is wrong with Matthew. My job is to diagnose and fix, and I haven't been able to do that."

Surprisingly, those words were reassuring to me, not because he couldn't tell me what was wrong but because I knew that he was totally committed to finding a resolution, and he was invested in Matthew's care. He stood up, stared at Matthew for a moment, and then turned to me and said, "I promise you that I won't stop looking until we find the answer."

As the hours passed, Matthew appeared to be in a near catatonic state. Motionless except when vomiting and mute, he made little eye contact. When he would look at me, his eyes spoke so deeply. I could see the hurt and fear in my sweet baby, and I was terrified. He never cried, never screamed, never asked why. He just processed it all internally. Through all of the pokes and prods, never once did he balk at something the nurses asked him to do. He just seemed to be slipping farther and farther away. The unknown underlying condition causing the high blood pressure was definitely taking its toll. We were so frightened that an answer would not come soon enough. He needed to have me constantly touching him for security. Hour after hour I held him and watched that monitor. I prayed silently the entire time for his healing, too scared that the sounds or volume of my voice would be too much for him to endure. I was praying for a miracle and that everything would return to normal.

I had been careful not to let Matthew see me cry. We tried to stay as composed as we could for his sake. But, out of fear, tiredness, and anxiety, I finally couldn't help the watershed. My eyes filled up and before I could stop them, the tears were streaming. I refused to sob, but I could not stop the tears. I thought about all that he was missing. I was pleading in my head with God to please give us an answer, give us some direction to turn. Not knowing any answers was torture. In those few brief minutes, I went from pleading with God for answers to being hurt and angry at God for letting this happen. Why? What had this innocent child ever done to deserve this?

If there has ever been a time that my faith and beliefs were tested, this was indeed the time. I collected my thoughts. *Look, girly, you have to get it back together. Now is not the time for anger or bitterness. Focus! He needs you!* I felt so helpless, and the feeling that God had abandoned us surged through me. *If he was truly with us, why can't he make it better? Why can't he at least show us an answer?* Still, through these difficult circumstances, I have learned *never* to question God's will or his timing. It is perfect in his plan. Everything truly happens for a reason.

The late evening brought a new direction—not miraculous healing news, but a definite step in a positive direction. One of his twenty-four hour urinalysis labs and one of the ultrasounds had come back with some evidence to indicate something may be wrong with his renal system. The doctors speculated that it preliminarily looked as though his right kidney was enlarged and his left kidney may have a kidney stone in it. There was relief! Kidney stone. Painful, yes. But definitely treatable. This was the first positive thing we had heard in nearly a week.

But the doctor went on to say that they could not rule out other more serious issues as well as disregard their initial suspicions. The only thing that was known for sure was that he needed specialized care and evaluation of his renal system. We were told that at the time there were no pediatric nephrologists (kidney doctors for kids) in Baton Rouge. The closest nephrology group was in New Orleans at the Children's Hospital. The doctor explained that he was on his way to consult with them for an immediate plan of action. This meant in all probability we would have to transfer to New Orleans. This was a huge change of the game. This would also mean no more evening drives home for Billy to be with Conner. It would essentially mean we would be temporarily and indefinitely be moving to the Children's Hospital.

Matthew's doctor returned and to say that after consulting with Children's Hospital, everyone was in agreement that he should be transferred. The necessary arrangements would be made, and everything would be put into motion early the next morning. Matthew would spend one more night in Baton Rouge, and then the next day we would head to the Crescent City.

ten

NO PRAYERS, PLEASE

Transport day had come. It could not have come soon enough. Matthew was frail and looked as though he was losing all of his fight. The necessary procedure to place a central line and reposition his arterial line required a team of professionals to complete, and as the doctors and nurses filled the room, the commotion intensified, and my apprehension hit its maximum. I should have been looking forward with optimism because we were closer to understanding why everything was happening. Instead, I felt as if a looming storm were on the horizon. I thought my body would explode with tears and grief. Then, just as the activity was ramping up and we were preparing to leave the room, we had another visitor—the interim pastor at our church. We had enjoyed the services she led during worship, but when I saw her at the hospital, I wanted to melt into the floor. I wanted to ask her to leave.

The rational side of me knew she was there to offer support and prayer. But the tired and anxious side of me thought the worst. Even though turning to God throughout the previous few days was the only thing I knew to do, I did not want her to pray with us right then. It was too formal. Somewhere deep within me, I feared she was there to give Matthew a final prayer. The sight of her conjured up negative thoughts of finality that I did not want to experience.

But I knew that within minutes Matthew would again be sedated for a serious procedure requiring great skill and finesse by the doctors. After a few deep breaths, I choked back my tears and put all of the emotions aside. Billy and I joined hands with her for a final prayer.

The prayers were sent up for God to lay his hand of protection on Matthew, for Billy and I to have strength, and to give Matthew comfort and peace. The following month we would learn just how profound these words would be. God did indeed hear them. Even in our darkest hours, he was always listening.

Now I find myself grateful beyond words or measure for that visit. When the events that would unfold over the course of the next hour or so were finally realized by our family, that prayer would become one of the greatest gifts anyone has ever given. The prayer was brief and soon after we finished, the doctors were ready to begin their procedure. They advised us that they didn't know how long it would take. The transport team from Children's Hospital arrived. A trauma nurse from the PICU was sent to go back to New Orleans with Matthew. The ambulance driver and the nurse gathered the necessary information as the doctors began working on Matthew.

Dawn had arrived with some food, and we made the long walk downstairs. I stirred around the mashed potatoes, not wanting to eat. Our hearts and attention were upstairs with Matthew. We waited about thirty minutes, then decided to go back to check on the status. We waited patiently for a few minutes until the information nurse allowed us to enter his room. We saw that the arterial line had been repositioned, and the central line was successfully placed in his groin. She said that he was still sedated but should be waking up shortly. I couldn't wait to get back to his side.

The ambulance driver was standing in the hall, waiting patiently. The trauma nurse from Children's said that as soon as Matthew was awake and the all clear was given with his vitals, they could be on their way. The nurses prepared him to be on the portable monitors. Billy, Dawn, and I were with him, and I gently stroked his sweet little head, waiting for him to wake up.

Within just a few minutes, he opened his eyes and looked up and said, "Hey, Mom!" He looked more awake and coherent than he had looked during the previous week. A huge smile came across my face when we saw him so lucid. There was *my* Matthew—the sweet little boy who had been fighting so hard the past few days. Billy began to tell him that he was going to ride with him in the ambulance to New Orleans. Though parents normally wouldn't be allowed to ride in the ambulance, after much debating and pleading, we were given special permission for Billy to go with Matthew. He had been so frightened to be alone the past week, and the emotions could have a devastating effect on his blood pressure and potentially put his life in danger. The doctors agreed that it was indeed in his best interest to have a parent with him so his blood pressure would not rise any higher.

For the first time since this ordeal began, I felt we would finally find answers, that we had turned a corner. The doctors in Baton Rouge assured us how skilled the nephrology team at Children's Hospital was. Matthew was coherent, and we would be in New Orleans within a couple of hours. Now all we needed was for the vomiting to stop completely and for his blood pressure to stabilize. I took a deep breath and soaked in those brief seconds as I listened to Billy assure Matthew of how fun the ambulance ride would be. Matthew even giggled, weakly, but from his heart. That quiet giggle was a welcome sound.

That feeling of bliss and hope abruptly ended. As we were continuing our quiet conversation, Matthew's eyes rolled back into his head. He became lethargic and unresponsive and then lost consciousness. I was in a state of disbelief and terror at what I just saw. We gently started calling his name and stroking his hands.

"Matthew. Come on, Matthew, wake up. Matthew, you need to open your eyes." With each call of his name, our level of anxiety edged up. Why wasn't he waking up? Time passed slowly. My heart raced. My knees began to felt like rubber, and I was sure all of the blood was draining from my body. Dawn soothingly told me to just breathe. The PICU doctor was notified of Matthew's condition and vitals, and she ran into the room. She walked out to the desk and called the PICU admitting doctor at Children's to let him know of the change in Matthew's status. Initially, we all held on to the hope that he had just simply went to sleep for a few more minutes. But the onset was sudden, and he did not even attempt to open his eyes.

By this point we were joined at Matthew's bedside by the nurse and the ambulance driver, who had tiptoed to the foot of his bed. She was gently wiggling Matthew's feet, even giving him promises of turning on the lights and sirens if he wanted to during the trip to New Orleans. We all felt panicked and uncertain.

I was shaking from head to toe. Fear was consuming me. *What if he didn't wake up?* We became more and more concerned. My gut told me this was not just a little boy who needed a nap. This was a little boy whose body was tired from the past week of fighting. Matthew's vitals and the color of his face and skin began to change.

One minute turned into two. Two minutes into three. Three minutes into four. In everyday life a couple of minutes doesn't seem like a long time to wait. But when you are praying, hoping, and pleading for your child to wake up, every minute becomes an eternity. My hope was ticking away with each second. I looked at Dawn, who was deeply concerned. She stepped aside so I could get even closer to Matthew's head. She urged me to tell him everything I wanted to say. This was serious. If until this point I had only experienced the panic of a worried mother, that had just changed.

I was on one side of Matthew's bed, and Billy was on the other. We were each holding his little hands. He felt so limp in our grasp. With tears rolling down our faces, we soothingly told him how much we loved him and how precious a gift he was to us. We told him he was a gift straight from God that we had prayed so desperately for. We told him how proud we were of him for just being Matthew. We desperately pleaded with him to open his eyes. *This can't be it. It is not time. His whole life has yet to be lived. He was not even five years old yet. This amazing, wonderful, loving, gifted, smart child had so much to give to the world.* I was angry with God and begged him to not do this. This can't be the path.

At that moment, I vowed to God that if he returned Matthew to us, I would do everything I could to serve him and give back to the world. I told God that I was completely surrendering to him, and all I asked in return was for my baby back. No words can truly express the gravity of emotion, pain, dread, and helplessness that rushed in that moment. The desperation was indescribable.

Then, miracles of all miracles, Matthew's beautiful green eyes slowly opened wide and bright. The collective sigh of relief must have been heard on the bottom floor. The tears started pouring. *Had this really happened? Oh, thank you, God!* Matthew looked up at me and said, "Mommy, why are you crying?" He looked around the room and wanted to know why everyone looked so sad.

A wave of gratitude poured through me. The feeling surpassed even what I felt when he was placed in my arms for the first time as a newborn. I knew that God's mercy had shined down on him, and the Great Physician and Magnificent Healer was at work. He had heard our prayers! He was listening! My beautiful child was once again with us. It would be weeks before I would fully understand just how far he had traveled. Through my tears, I gave him a big smile and asked,

"Baby, did you have a nice nap?" Not fully wanting an answer, I felt something needed to be said to break the solemn mood. He just smiled. I quickly stroked his head, and his daddy looked as though a load of bricks had just been removed from his chest.

Billy and I looked at each other and knew what had just happened was profound. I remember thinking, *You knew all along that something was not right, Billy. Your instincts were spot on.*

The unresponsive episode was noted in his chart as lasting five to ten minutes. It could have just as easily said thirty years. Once his status was improved, a nurse called Children's Hospital to let them know that Matthew had indeed made it and was on his way. The nurses made the final preparations to get him on the stretcher. Billy followed the stretcher out, and they were on their way. When they left the room, I collapsed on his bed, that same bed he had been confined to for the past five days. The same bed that I nearly saw him take his last breath just a few minutes earlier. I was completely overcome. Dawn wrapped her arms around me. Even the charge nurse, who had become such a rock to me over the past week, hugged me tightly and assured me it would be okay. She said Matthew was a fighter, and he was not done.

Everything moved quickly after he was stabilized and ready to go. We had reached the turning point in what appeared like a stagnant cycle of no answers, no prognosis, and no path to get him better. It would be weeks before any discussion or thought of the events that had just happened would be mentioned again. Once Matthew arrived in New Orleans, doctors ran more tests to determine what had exactly happened earlier and if that factored into his care at Children's. But after everything was evaluated in the early hours of his arrival, this episode would be pushed to the back of our minds. All we knew was Matthew was awake and stable, and we were ready for a diagnosis. Almost a month later, we learned just what Matthew experienced on that amazing April day.

eleven

NEW ORLEANS

P oor little Conner's whole world was in complete turmoil. Conner was still staying with my parents and was being given all of the love and care humanly possible. But this would not replace having his family home. Even at two years old, he was keenly aware that things were not right. I had to spend time with Conner before I went to New Orleans. We knew that once we got there, the hospital would become our home for an undetermined amount of time because we still did not have an answer as to why Matthew was sick.

Conner ran up to me with the tightest hug imaginable. Oh, how I had missed this precious boy. I needed to take care of a thousand things before leaving but they could all be done with Conner in tow. The first thing we did was go into Matthew's room and get on our knees beside his bed and pray to God to heal and protect Matthew, and for Conner to feel the love of Jesus while we were gone. He even agreed to momentarily remove the pacifier from his mouth to help me pray. The image of that precious boy on his knees with his hands clasped makes my heart so full. He prayed for his big brother to feel better soon.

The immediate task at hand was to look up the address for the hospital in New Orleans. After getting an idea of direction and packing up some things, I walked back to my parents, and my immediate family gathered on the back porch. I remember my daddy sitting in the swing with tears in his eyes and asking me if Matthew was going to be okay. Trying to be strong for your own self-preservation is one thing, but to see your parents so vulnerable and wanting to keep them positive is another. My updates to them had been sporadic at best during the past week. I explained to them all that I knew up that point, which still wasn't much.

After spending some time with my family, I needed to take care of some errands, since I had no idea when Billy or I would be back. Dawn told me that she would help me with my errands, and then she would drive me to New Orleans. She arrived at my house, and we loaded up Conner and went to grab some dinner. After eating and taking care of the errands, we brought Conner back to my parents, and I said my tearful good-bye. We set off for the sixty-mile drive to New Orleans. I don't remember much of the trip since I was constantly worrying about Matthew.

Billy called me to let me know they had made it safely, and Matthew was admitted to the PICU. Doctors were performing tests, and Billy hoped that by the time I got there the next morning, we could move forward. The plan was for me to check into a local hotel close to the hospital and spend the night. Early the next morning Dawn would bring me to the hospital during the nurses shift change. Billy and I could switch off, and he could go to the hotel and sleep for a while. Dawn and I arrived at the hotel, and for the first time in five days, I managed to sleep for a couple of hours. Being away from Matthew was torture, but I knew my body could only go for so long without sleep. As I drifted off, I prayed vigilantly for God to please help our son. I was ready to go early the next morning and get to Matthew's side. We needed answers to why he had become so sick and why his life was in jeopardy, but I also kept replaying the episode that happened in Baton Rouge. Why had he gone unconscious, and why had it looked like he was drifting away from us?

I'll never forget visiting Children's Hospital for the first time. Billy met me and Dawn by the front desk and slowly walked us to the cafeteria, giving me the layout of what he knew about the place so far. We walked past the PICU, and he explained to me where Matthew's bed was. Over a donut, he conveyed to me how different this environment was from what we had left in Baton Rouge. The severity of the patients was much more intense, and the PICU was much more compact. But he reassured me that the team of physicians had been on top of Matthew's case from the moment he arrived and that we would get the results of the CT scan of his brain soon.

After Billy was done explaining, Dawn took him to the hotel so he could rest. Then she headed back home. Hotels in New Orleans are not cheap, and even though we were staying at one of the most plain and simple hotels in the city, it would be quite expensive to stay there. Not knowing how long we would be there, this was a definite concern. Since Matthew was in the PICU, we couldn't keep our belongings anywhere except in the waiting room across the hall. This was not secure by any means, and the waiting room wasn't exactly an environment that someone would feel comfortable sleeping in. The beds in the PICU had one rolling chair next to them for a parent to sit in. Until Matthew was in a regular room, our situation would be costly and uncomfortable.

Before Matthew got sick, I had never really given any serious thought to how much life is impacted by having a tragedy such as illness, especially given that many times patients are transferred to hospitals away from their homes in order to receive care for their condition. It was another of God's great lessons for me to understand the plight of others during stressful times. I have come to appreciate the gravity of change that comes with unfortunate circumstances.

twelve

GOD WILL NOT FAIL US

I walked into the PICU, hoping to see progress in Matthew's care. Within the first half hour a neurologist came in and explained that a CT scan of Matthew's brain was done the evening before to try and determine what happened to him in Baton Rouge. She said that she had reviewed the study, and, after going over all of the data, she did not see any evidence of a stroke, seizure, or coma, which was initially suspected. She said that his brain looked perfect. All of the gray matter looked as the doctors would anticipate it to look.

This was great news, but I was frustrated because it still did not give a concrete explanation as to what happened in Baton Rouge. I asked her what had caused that episode of unconsciousness. I was there and knew what I witnessed. It was not a fainting spell. Her reply was that she had no medical explanation for what had happened, even after going over his full case. I pushed her further. After all, she was a doctor, and I was tired of hearing nothing and no answers. There had to be a reason for what happened. Then in a completely unexpected response, she looked me right in the eye and asked me if I believed. Of course I believe! That is the only thing keeping me going. I didn't think twice to ask her what it was she was asking me I *believed* in. I just assumed God.

She said, "Well, then you may want to send up an extra prayer of thanks the next time you talk to him." *Was this really her answer?*

The doctor continued, "Sometimes there is just not a scientific or medical explanation that can be given in some cases. I believe that in some cases there is a much higher power at work than what medicine and doctors can take credit for." And with that she smiled graciously and walked off.

This conversation went nothing like I anticipated it would. The event had gone through my mind many times in the hours before. I pondered the doctor's words for a few minutes, then said a quick word of thanks. I was grateful that Matthew's brain was perfect, but I knew we had more worries to contend with. We needed an answer and game plan to correct Matthew's life-threatening blood pressures. There was no way I wanted him to experience another episode like what had happened the day before.

Later, a social worker who worked at the hospital, introduced herself, got the full story about Matthew, and gave me information about the Ronald McDonald House in New Orleans and their services to patient's families. We made a few phone calls, and within the hour, Billy was checking out of the hotel and moving our things to the Ronald McDonald House. Billy would stay during the day and be at the hospital for 6:00 a.m. shift change, and I would then leave and go grab a few hours of sleep and come back for the night shift. As dire as the situation was, there was finally some hope to some of the hurdles we faced.

Now that we had received good news in the fact that Matthew had not suffered a stroke or seizure, the task at hand was to find out what was wrong with him. There was a constant stream of doctors and nurses, and we finally met the physician who would give us an answer to what was plaguing our sweet child.

After additional radiology and lab studies, the doctors concluded that Matthew was born with a condition called renal artery stenosis.

It was a blockage to the main artery that feeds the blood supply to his left kidney. The lack of sufficient blood caused his renin level to increase and, therefore, caused him to have high blood pressure. The slight loss of blood during the outpatient surgery to put tubes in his ears and tonsillectomy would usually not be a life-changer for most kids. But in Matthew's case, the tiny amount of blood loss combined with the high blood pressure already present caused his renin level to skyrocket, and his kidney sent a signal to his brain that it needed more blood to function. The higher-than-normal blood pressure shot to dangerous levels to compensate for a lack of blood to the kidney. However, we had no idea he was suffering from hypertension at the time of surgery because he had never had routine blood pressure screens.

Now that we knew what was causing all of this to happen, the doctors needed to figure out how to fix it. Within a week or so, the PICU physicians and nephrologists found the right balance of medications that would control his blood pressure at levels that would allow him to be admitted to a regular room on one of the patient floors of the hospital. As things progressed, Matthew slowly began to eat again. What a welcome sight. Even though he was exhausted and still sick, he was improving.

Moving day to the other floor came on Easter Sunday of 2007. What a surprise I got when I woke up at the Ronald McDonald House and called to check on him. Billy shared the exciting news about the room change. I was already excited about the day because I was going to see Conner and my mom. Dawn was driving them to New Orleans to spend some time with us on Easter. When they arrived to pick me up, I was beyond excited and couldn't wait to get to the hospital. Seeing Matthew in a regular room without the sights and sounds of the PICU was a gift. I felt so thankful that God was working through Matthew and was continuing to bless him. Even then we still did not know how much God had touched his young life.

The next couple of weeks went by with continued improvement. As doctors continued to consult with one another about how to best fix the blockage, Matthew finally reached a point where he was well enough to go home. We were told that Matthew needed invasive vascular bypass surgery, but his body was not well enough at the time to endure that type of serious procedure. Another more temporary measure must be explored. His doctor said that they would like to attempt a balloon angioplasty done during an angiogram in order to give that artery some relief. The tricky part was finding an interventional radiologist willing to tackle this in a child's kidney. Apparently, this is not an easy task. We were discharged with instructions to continue his daily blood pressure readings and medications and to expect a call within the next few days with information about the angiogram.

Matthew came home a different child than he was prior to March 28. Always having been a very deep child, he seemed somehow different. As expected, he was still continuing to heal and recover, but he appeared to have the weight of the world on his shoulders. It was something that I could never quite put my finger on exactly. My mother's intuition was telling me something was troubling my little one.

thirteen

MOM'S BIBLE

The call came about the angiogram and the procedure was scheduled for the end of April. An interventional radiologist at East Jefferson Hospital in New Orleans was willing to take on this complicated task. We were grateful beyond measure that someone was found to attempt the procedure.

The early morning of April 27, 2007, found us in New Orleans again. Going through admissions and pre-op was fairly easy. We were praying the procedure to open the blockage was just as uncomplicated. As Matthew was being prepped, he looked nervous and was fighting back tears.

With all of the strength he could muster, he asked, "Mommy, am I going to die today?"

I remember thinking, *What would make him ask me this?*

I replied, "Baby, no one is dying today. You be brave, and I will see you as soon as the doctor is finished. I love you!" With that, I bent down and kissed his sweet cheek. My heart sank into my toes. I couldn't imagine why he had such a thought.

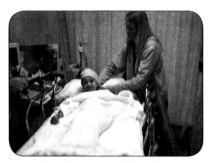

"Am I going to die today,
Mommy?"

When the procedure was completed, we were told that Matthew indeed had a 99 percent occlusion to the main artery that feeds blood supply to his kidney. The doctor said it was amazing that his kidney had not died already, with only 1 percent open for blood to get in. This would account for the small size of the kidney as compared to his right. The radiologist was only able to open it by about 50 percent. Pushing it any further would risk rupture and require emergency surgery that we all knew his body could not handle. The temporary fix was in place, and we prayed for it to buy Matthew some time, so to speak. Maybe until he was nine or ten, we hoped.

For another week Matthew was a patient in the hospital for monitoring, so his blood pressure medications could safely be adjusted to compensate for the increased blood flow to his kidney. During this week he remained quiet and looked as though he was in deep thought most of the time. I would often ask him if everything was okay, trying to give him an opportunity to express his feelings. We knew early on that this experience was going to affect him deeply, and we wanted to make sure his emotions had a way to heal just like his body. But we knew this would come with time.

Matthew's class at school was preparing for their end-of-the-year graduation celebration. Having missed nearly two months of school and knowing it would be impossible for him to return before classes ended, we were thankful when his teacher said she still wanted him to be a part of the program. Even if he wasn't up to the standing and singing, he could sit on stage with them. A week before the ceremony we went to school so he could see his classmates, and they could all see him to know he was okay. I never knew that a sick classmate could leave a lasting impression on some children until I brought Matthew back to class. It was important for them to know that he was getting better. He enjoyed seeing everyone, and I took pictures to capture it. Matthew still has one of those pictures hanging on his bedroom door. The photo was special to him, and he later told me that he had always felt loved and safe in that classroom. In the time he visited, they sang a couple of songs and did a little prayer before we left.

I could still tell that something was bothering Matthew, but he was still not ready to share it. Assuming that he would share or ask questions about his ordeal when he was ready, I didn't push. Honestly, the daily activity of blood pressure measurements every two hours, three different medications around the clock, a low sodium diet, and the efforts to return to a sense of normalcy back in our lives were consuming.

One afternoon following his visit to school, we were playing on the floor with Conner when Matthew had an unusual request. He asked for me to read from the Bible. He had always liked story books, but it was different for him to ask for a reading from the Bible. At the time we were Christians who put God first and prayed regularly, attended church a couple of times out of the month, and taught our children that God has divine power. But we were not a family that regularly read scriptures at home to our children. We would share stories or events from the Bible that coincided with stories Matthew may have learned from school, but that was about all we did. I found it odd that Matthew would request for me to read from the Bible.

I went to his room and grabbed his children's Bible from his bookshelf. If he wanted to hear God's word, I would do it. After I sat down on the couch, Matthew said, "No, Mom, I want you to read from *your* Bible." After a brief pause, I exchanged the books and sat down again.

I said, "Okay, here it is." He gave a huge smile. I asked, "Where do you want to start?" I honestly had no idea which scripture or book to read from. I wasn't sure what was troubling his heart at that moment, but thought that maybe text regarding healing and God's power to make the sick well would be something appropriate. All the while I was pondering how I would put the formal words from the pages into language that Matthew would understand. Matthew took the book, opened it, and pointed firmly at what he wanted me to read. It was from the book of John. John 3:16 to be exact. *For God so loved the world, that he gave his only begotten Son, that whosoever believeth in him should not perish, but have everlasting life.* He looked completely content after I finished the sentence. I was puzzled, surprised, and amazed all at once.

I asked, "Matthew, do you understand what those words mean?"

He looked at me like I had completely lost my mind and said, "Of course, Mom! Do you know what they mean?"

I giggled and said, "Well, I'm not sure. Can you help me out and explain it?" He proudly sat up with his little Hot Wheels car in his hand and gave me an explanation that God loves each of us so much that he sent his very own Son to die on the cross for all of the bad things we have each done.

He asked, "Mommy, do you know what sin is?"

"Yes, it is when we do something wrong or bad that God would not like," I replied.

He smiled again and, with the amusement of a teacher whose student just answered the most difficult of questions, gave me a huge hug.

After that he went back to playing with Conner and their cars. I sat there for a few minutes watching them playing. Confused was an understatement. It was hard to process what had just happened. Why did Matthew ask for me to read from the Bible? Why did he choose that one verse out all the others? Was it a complete coincidence? The boys giggled and roared their cars around the floor.

The routine of the day continued, and after everyone was tucked safely into bed, I recounted to myself what had taken place earlier in the afternoon. I felt immense pride in the fact that my child had felt in his heart the desire to turn to God's word, but exactly why did it happen at that moment? And, again, why those words? Especially given that at this point it was not a routine occurrence they would have witnessed in our home. Prayers to the heavens had just brought us through the darkest point in our lives, and we remembered to give thanks for the blessings. I didn't want to make a big deal out of the conversation with Matthew. I just assumed it may have been a passing occurrence. Nothing could prepare us for the coming revelation Matthew would give testimony to.

fourteen

THE EYES OF A CHILD

Matthew's eyes always held a depth that went straight to his soul. Since coming home from the hospital, his eyes appeared to be filled with so much more. We weren't sure if it was sadness or worry on his part—probably a combination of the two. Matthew is an intelligent child, almost too smart sometimes. His intelligence has made his life as a child difficult many times. It is hard to have lost so much and be forced to mature in ways unthinkable for most parents, while at the same time still trying to just fit in with other kids his age. So much of his childhood was torn away from him in a matter of weeks.

His life, as he knew it and as we dreamed it, was forever changed. The thoughts of him playing T-ball and soccer had vanished. His body was nowhere near a point that he could exert himself on those levels. Instead we hoped for a different and renewed path for him that would still bring fulfillment and enjoyment much like most little boys experience from sports. Anything that Matthew did had to be undertaken with caution, knowing that too much exertion or not enough fluid could lead to disastrous consequences. This was not an easy task as we were heading into the summer in South Louisiana. The temperatures can be brutal for healthy people, much less those with health concerns.

As Matthew continued to get stronger, we would take evening breaks outside to enjoy the weather before it became so unbearable we couldn't stand it. One evening we went outside, and I found a comfy spot on our swing. Matthew and Conner settled into the area of dirt right off our back steps to begin rolling their dump trucks. I quietly watched them. I have learned to relish moments like these. No talking, no plans, just simply watching and taking in what is so precious in my mind. Just a few weeks earlier, we had longed to have them playing together just like this. Now those prayers were answered, and my boys were together again. My heart was content.

After a few minutes of playing, Matthew quietly got up and walked a few feet toward the end of our driveway. He sat down with his back to us. I don't think he even realized I was still in the swing. Carefully watching for a minute or so, I was curious about what he was doing. Initially, I thought he just needed a break and may have gotten tired. He learned early on that Conner was acutely aware of his health condition, and even at such a young age, he did his best to shield his little brother from seeing too much of it. If he needed a break or felt bad, he would always try to go where Conner could not see.

After a bit I walked over to him and kneeled down beside him. He looked up at me with the most resolute expression. It was as though he wanted or needed to say something so badly but just couldn't bring himself to do it.

I asked, "Is anything wrong, buddy?"

He just stared at me with a look of deep thought in his eyes and said, "No, everything is okay." He assured me he felt okay and said he just needed to take a break. I gently asked again if he was all right, and he said yes. After a few minutes, he got back up and joined Conner again in the dirt.

After Billy got home, I shared the events of the afternoon with him. Our hearts ached for this little boy and all he had gone through, and we struggled with ways to make ourselves understand. We knew that Matthew and Conner needed us now more than they ever had in their lives as we struggled to put the pieces back together. We prayed things would continue in this way for a long time, and then we could deal with it as it came. But, without healing now, how would we ever endure another blow like we had just experienced?

The trauma seemed to be having a profound effect on Matthew. I rationalized that Matthew may have needed additional time to rest and recuperate. After all, it had been a long ordeal for him to endure, and it had taken a major toll on his body. I gave every assurance to Matthew that we were there to listen if he wanted to talk. He needed to talk, but he had to do it when he was ready. I was sure he would have questions about why this had happened to him, what had caused it, what the future held, and so on.

After dinner was finished, I was cleaning up, and Matthew walked to bring me his plate. I could still see that his face was deep in thought. I stooped down again in front of him, told him that I loved him, and kissed him on the forehead to give him every assurance that if he had questions or needed to talk, I was there to listen. He just nodded his head and his eyes looked like they were filling with tears again.

fifteen

A WALK WITH THE ANGELS

After bath time, we settled down to watch TV before bed-time. Around 8:00 p.m., Conner was asleep on my lap, so I scooped him up and brought him to his room. After returning to the living room, I found the TV off, and Matthew sitting quietly by himself on the couch. Billy was getting ready for bed. This was a welcome opportunity to spend a few quiet minutes with my buddy. I snuggled down next to him, pulled him close, and just hugged him. We sat there and said nothing. Matthew turned to face me, and there was that look in his eyes again—a look of so much that he needed to get out.

Before I could say anything, he said, "Mom, I need to tell you something, but you have to promise not to get mad."

I jokingly laughed and said, "I don't think there is anything under the sun you could do that would upset me." I pleaded with him to please tell me what was troubling him. Then it started. He said that he went somewhere without my permission. I could think of nowhere he had gone that I didn't know about, especially the past few months. He was always a child who would tell on himself if he did something wrong, but I couldn't imagine he was pondering about something from before he got sick. Nothing seemed serious enough to make him so distressed.

The next sentence from his mouth will be ingrained in my brain forever. Matthew looked up at me and said, "Mommy, please don't get mad, but four angels came to get me when I was sick." *Oh my word!* What had he just said? Before he explained any further, I told him to hold that thought and calmly walked to the back of the house to get Billy.

"You need to come hear this," I said. I wasn't sure what else he was going to say, but I knew that I needed Billy to be present. I didn't tell Billy what Matthew had just said. We returned to the living room, and we both sat down with Matthew. We remained calm and unaffected. Billy had no idea what had happened, and I did not want Matthew to see any reaction from me.

"Okay, Matthew. Can you tell Daddy what you just told me?" Peering at Billy, he said, "Daddy, you can't get mad either." Billy was not sure what was happening. He assumed one of the toy Hot Wheels may have scratched the floor or something was broken.

Matthew repeated, "Four angels came to get me when I was sick in the hospital." Though I had not spoken a word to Billy to remind him to remain calm, he instinctively sat with a poker face. Neither of us spoke. We waited for Matthew to share more if he wanted.

The most beautiful, magnificent story of a path to heaven was laid out before us with the grace, eloquence, and verbalization that would be expected from someone three times Matthew's age.

"I saw a very gray door and turned the handle. Once the door opened, there was the most beautiful, bright, white light that my eyes have ever seen. I stood for just a minute, and there were four angels that were standing in front of me—two men and two women. I think they were angels because they were wearing pretty white robes," he said.

As the words poured from Matthew's mouth, Billy and I sat stunned. We were completely blindsided by what we were hearing. Neither of us wanted to prod, and our parenting instincts kicked in to let him elaborate on his own terms. This was something he needed to share in his own way with his own words and descriptions.

"One of the ladies bent down and told me it was time to come with them. She was a much older lady, but she made me feel safe. I told her that I can't go with them because I haven't asked my mom and dad. She smiled at me and told me it was okay because you guys already knew that I was going to be walking with them."

This was powerful. With each sentence Matthew shared, it was as though we could see the load lifting off of his little soul. As he realized he was not in trouble and we were not mad, he shared freely about this incredible experience.

Matthew continued, "After she told me that you guys knew and it was okay, I felt like I was supposed to go. I felt totally safe with them. Two angels got on each side of me and I was in the middle. We all held hands. The older lady was on my right and the older man was on my left. When they grabbed my hands, I felt so much love."

The words were so commanding. I needed to hear more and was trying to remain unruffled. Was it a glimpse into heaven? Was he walking the path to Jesus?

Matthew continued, "As we held hands, the older lady looked down with a smile and asked if I was ready. I nodded my head yes, and we started slowly walking. Everything was white, white, white! The robes, road, and everything around us was just a beautiful white. The further we walked, the better I felt. It was just love, Mom! I didn't see anyone else other than the people with me. I never asked where we were going because I felt safe. There was a feeling that we were going to a great place, and I was excited about it, even though I didn't know where it was. As we walked the path, the white around us became even prettier and brighter. Then after a few minutes, we all stopped. The older lady looked down at me and smiled again. She said that it was time to stop walking and I needed to go back. I didn't want to come back. It was so pretty that I wanted to stay. Please, please don't be mad at me, Mommy, because I wanted to stay."

Matthew was holding my hand by this point, and I squeezed his hand as if to say it was all right because I understood. Fighting every emotion that was rolling over us, Billy and I still did not speak.

Matthew continued, "The older lady told me that I could not stay this time. She said that you and Daddy needed me after all and that I had to go back. Even though I felt sad, I listened to what she said. The two angels let go of my hand, and she put her hand on my shoulder and turned me around. I was facing the same direction where we started. She said she would see me again one day, but until then I had other things to do. Then I started the walk back by myself. It was still really bright and white. The more I walked, the less bright it was. Then I saw the same gray door from earlier. The door was still open, and I just walked through it. The next thing I remember is you and Daddy looking at me and crying in my hospital room. Then I left with Daddy in the ambulance."

Had I really just heard all of that? When Matthew finished, it was as though we had been holding our breath the entire time. Billy and I exhaled slowly and deeply and looked at each other with confusion in our eyes, trying to understand if all of that meant what we thought it meant.

Matthew asked, "Are you mad, Mom?" I hugged him as tightly as I could and gave him every assurance that I was not mad. Then he asked me the toughest question I will probably ever be asked:

"Mom, does that mean I died?"

Nowhere in the deepest parts of my imagination could I have ever thought that my innocent child would be asking this question of me. I knew that he wanted an answer, but nothing could have prepared me to give one. I slowly began to look for the right words that would let him know that we gave credit to his account and validate what he recalled but to also let him know that God was the only authority on this matter.

Until this point in Matthew's life, we had never had a discussion of death or any detailed descriptions of heaven. All of his grandparents were still alive, and we had not lost anyone close to our family. Honestly, after the experience at the hospital and the neurologist ruling out anything serious, death was never thought of or discussed again. We put those fears away and focused on the daily aspects of keeping him healthy and putting our lives back together. I would have never imagined that something so deep and powerful had transformed his soul during that event.

I asked Matthew what he thought the experience meant. His reply was simply, "I think I was dying, and the angels were bringing me to Jesus."

These powerful and insightful words shook me to my foundation. My explanation was that God would be the only person who could ever truly know if that meant he was dying. One day he would be in the kingdom of heaven, and he could ask that very question. From what I have always been taught, heard, or read, nearly everything of what he said mirrored accounts of glimpses into what we think of heaven. Billy and I both knew in our hearts what it all meant. We had been on the other end witnessing what was happening to his physical body, and we remembered the consuming fear we had of just what he was describing. We never truly imagined that he would have had such a prevailing experience that would make him feel like he was dying. When he woke up from those frightful minutes of unconsciousness in the hospital, I jokingly asked him if he'd had a nice nap. I was not really looking for an answer; it was just a question to break the tension we all felt.

Had this been the source of the deep thoughts and distant behavior since coming home? It would certainly warrant a change of behavior and a bit of retrospection. Here I sat as a grown woman trying to understand what Matthew had said and believing that my child had truly been on a path to see Jesus. We have heard accounts of the magnificence that awaits us at the time of death from a fortunate few, but to have my own child recounting what his little eyes saw firsthand was beyond words. The words he used so vividly described the absolute splendor. How can being a child in a strange place with people you have never met make you feel safe? Why would he say it simply just felt like *love*? Furthermore, what would make him say that he felt like he was dying and was going to meet Jesus?

The three of us sat on the couch holding each other. We asked Matthew if he ever felt scared during the entire time. He replied, "No, not at all! I felt so safe and happy."

"Matthew, if what happened meant you were going to see Jesus, I am very grateful that God decided it was not your time to be in his kingdom. This means that God has great purpose for your life here on earth, and you are destined to do great things," I explained.

At that moment he hugged me so tightly, and we all began to cry and felt an emotional release of not only the account he just shared but also of the tragedy and tiredness of the past month and a half of our upside-down world. After we were all composed, it was time for bed.

Matthew brushed his teeth, and I tucked him in. Before I left his room, he told me that he felt relieved that he had been able to finally get all of that out. Billy and I walked back down the hall to our room and collapsed on the bed, still shocked about at what Matthew had told us. There was never a question of whether or not we believed him. It was just a matter of how could we put all of this into perspective and let him continue to heal. We decided to just let everything ride for a while and see if he mentioned it again. For the time being, our main focus was his health and the daily aspects of continuing his healing. As I closed my eyes that night, I envisioned the scene Matthew had painted for us with his words. How totally and amazingly beautiful it was! I knew he was witness to the splendor that is God's work and miracles. Then the hair on the back of my neck raised because his experience gave evidence to just how closely we had come to losing our precious baby boy.

sixteen

MAKING SENSE
OF IT ALL

I t was another absolutely breathtaking May morning in south Louisiana. Spring brought with it the newness of flowers blooming and nature coming to life after the mild winter. Our morning started the same as every other since returning from the hospital—blood pressure reading, medications, breakfast, and dressing for the day. Once the boys were up and ready, we made our way to my parents' house. As always, the boys bounced right in the door without giving any thought to formalities of knocking. Matthew's detailed account that he had shared the night before was pressing on my mind. Normally, I would run to the phone and call my mother immediately to share such an event. But I needed some time to digest what I heard. After processing it, I knew that I needed to tell my mom. Hugs and kisses were exchanged between my mom and dad from the boys. They were excited to see Maw Maw and Ghe Ghe.

The boys settled into playing in the living room and entertaining my daddy for a bit. Mom and I strolled out to the back porch swing. There was no right or wrong way to tell her what I needed to say, so out it came. It just spilled out before I could help it. I gave a play-by-play of all that Matthew had vividly told us. It was engraved in my brain at this point because it had been replayed in my mind hundreds of times in the past few hours.

There were immediate tears in her eyes. She knew exactly what we knew. This child had been on the brink of leaving us forever. It felt as though an airplane had just taken off from my shoulders when I finished.

She looked at me and said as she choked back tears, "God wasn't ready for him. His work has not yet been done here." This was an emotional experience, and she was right there for me just as she had done my entire life. Just as Matthew had needed me, I needed her in this time.

We discussed the experience a bit more and then the boys bounced out the back door, ready to play in the yard before lunch-time. They headed straight to their trucks and their favorite dirt hole near the back steps. Not exactly the finest landscaping in that small area, but it was a spot of land filled with the laughter and love of little boys playing with trucks. Billy and I decided this would be their play area until they were too big for trucks in the dirt. Our swing was positioned so that we could sit in the afternoons and enjoy watching them play with all of the innocence of childhood. So much of this had been robbed from them in the past couple of months. We tried never to take it for granted before, but now these times held an even deeper passion in our hearts to savor every single minute of their childhoods.

As we prepared to head back home for Matthew's afternoon dose of medicines, I told my mom that if Matthew wanted to talk about his experiences further, I would be open to it, but we did not plan to dwell on what he had said. There was still too much other physical healing that needed to be done. I knew we just needed to continue to count our blessings and be thankful for the extra opportunity afforded to us to have Matthew home and improving as we waited for the next hail storm to come our way. We didn't know when or how it would present, but the doctors were careful to impress upon us that the angioplasty procedure was only temporary. How long temporary played out was totally up to Matthew's body.

Watching Matthew go about his day and interact with Conner, Matthew appeared much more like his old self that day. He seemed more comfortable than in the previous days since coming home. Had his revelation really been burdening his soul so deeply? This was the first day that he seemed to not have the worries of the world on his shoulders. The need and desire to communicate and talk about issues is something that Billy and I have instilled in our children from their earliest teachings. We wanted them to know that it is always okay to talk to us or to anyone they are comfortable with, as long as their problems are communicated.

I was proud of Matthew for being so brave to discuss something so deep with us. This was obviously a subject that he realized in his young years was quite serious, and he wanted to have open ears and open minds for validation. Matthew could've carried these feelings with him, and manifest into other negative displays of attempted communication. Our wish was to always have an open and honest rapport with our boys.

Hoping that the events of the past twenty-four hours had helped alleviate some of Matthew's worries of how we would react, we let things move on as God had planned. Our ears and hearts were open if he needed to talk. At bedtime, he did mention it again as I tucked him in, he had a look of extreme happiness on his face. I couldn't help but smile back at him.

When I asked him what that smile was for, he said with so much conviction, "Mommy it was so, so beautiful." Not really sure exactly what he meant, I asked what specifically was so pretty.

"Heaven, Mommy!" Again, I was taken aback but immediately realized I could not show this in my face. I wanted him to feel like he could have the comfort of knowing I was okay with him discussing it.

There was so much enthusiasm in his voice. His expression showed he had more he wanted to share. "Mommy, do you think it was heaven?" Searching for the right answer, I simply stated that none of us can truly know if it was heaven.

"God is the only one who can answer that question for us. Matthew, do you believe in your heart it was heaven?"

"Mom, there is no place on earth that is as pretty as what I saw. This had to be heaven." He spoke these words with so much determination. "Mommy, I didn't really want to come back. I hope you're not mad. I love you and Daddy and Conner very much, but it was so perfect there that I didn't want to leave."

My knees grew weak at that statement. Matthew kept on surprising me with his insight. Could it be that this journey of his soul was truly the path to heaven? And if so, was it so magnificent that those who witness it really don't want to return?

"Matthew, I know that you love us and you do not need to feel bad because you thought heaven was so perfect you wanted to stay. Buddy, I'm so happy you did return. I'm grateful the angels gave you the message that you needed to come back to Mommy and Daddy."

With that, he smiled and gave me a hug.

Feeling as though we could look to the future in a positive way for the first time in months, I knew that we had other pressing events to plan: a promised trip to the beach and a fifth birthday party! As I lay in bed that night trying to decompress from the activity of the day, I began to think about some of the more difficult days and nights in the hospital when Matthew needed something positive to focus on. I would soothingly talk to him, and we would describe the serenity of being on a beach at sunset after a day of playing. We would talk about how the sand would feel between our toes or how the sun would dance down the horizon as night would fall. The peaceful sound of the waves as they would crash against the shore. How the serene sky would be filled with the colors of evening.

This technique was beneficial when he would begin to feel sad. He was anxious about the angiogram to balloon his renal artery and so were his daddy and I. As soon as the nurse placed the surgical cap on his head, his eyes looked like oceans filling with water. Not a sobbing cry but uncontrollable tears that inadvertently sneak up on us when we try to maintain composure. He tried to be brave, but he was as afraid.

"Matthew, where is our happy place?" We tried to help calm some of his anxieties before he was whisked off with the anesthesiologist and nurse.

"The beach!" Matthew's reply was quite somber: "Can we please go to the beach when all of this is over with? I want to *really* feel the sand in my toes." How could I not want to give him that request after all of the pain and agony this innocent child had endured?

"Matthew, as soon as this is over, we are heading to the beach! You will have sand between your toes," I replied. I had no idea how we would be able to keep our promise of his first beach trip financially, medically, or time wise, but we had to find a way.

Since that conversation that morning about a beach trip, we had not given much serious thought to the subject. That night, as I replayed the conversation in my mind, I knew that Billy and I needed to discuss it the next day and get plans underway. It was time for things to begin to get back to normal, and the boys needed to have something positive to look forward to. For the first time in so many long nights, I closed my eyes, feeling peace and optimism dancing in my heart. Things were finally settling into a comfortable, new normal and life felt more serene than it had in weeks.

seventeen

SUN, SAND, AND SOUL!

After researching room rates and dates, we were pleased to find a condo on the Gulf of Mexico in Orange Beach, Alabama, for nearly half of what they normally rent for. The few days we spent together as a family were so fulfilling. It was a time of renewal and reconnection. All of those nights Matthew and I spent in the hospital painting pictures in our mind of our "happy place" and he was finally able to see the splendor for himself. My brother had been working in Florida for a while and was on his way back to Louisiana. After a brief phone

Conner and Matthew
on the beach, 2007

conversation, he decided to take a detour and join us for a couple of days before he completed his trip home. It was a welcome experience, and I couldn't stop thanking God for all of the immeasurable gifts he had given to us.

On one of the evenings. I dressed the boys in their Easter outfits that they had never gotten to wear together because Matthew was in the hospital. We headed to the sand. One of my most treasured pictures was taken at sunset on the beach. Matthew and Conner were holding hands and staring out into the water. I had wanted to take some natural pictures of them just being boys, and this was what they instinctively did. This picture symbolized us as a family trying to regain some perspective.

The week at the beach went by quickly, and it was soon time to return to reality. We returned home to an eerie calm. We were relieved that things were stable with Matthew's health, but we held our breath as though we were just waiting for the next ball to drop. We knew his procedure was only a temporary measure, and it did not come with any time guarantees. Who knew when the next turning point would come? I resolved to not let this interfere with our everyday lives. We had to live with some sense of normalcy. Not just for Matthew and Conner but for all of us. My prayers were much of the same each day. For Matthew to live as normal a life

Matthew and Mr. Chad, 2007

as possible and continue to thrive and grow. I trusted that God had it all under control.

Part of getting our lives put back together was planning ahead for our next big event—Matthew's fifth birthday! Apparently, there had already been some planning on his part and that of one of his favorite nurses, Mr. Chad. During Matthew's

time in the PICU at Children's, he
was fortunate enough to receive
care from some of the most skilled
health care professionals. One of
his new friends was Mr. Chad, as
he became known by our family.
Chad helped ease Matthew's mind
by having conversations about
anything he thought would spark
Matthew's interest, from movies to
cars to birthdays.

When we started discussing
birthday party locations with Matthew, he informed me that he had
talked to Mr. Chad about it. They
thought it would be fun to have it

Matthew and Mr. Chad at
Matthew's fifth birthday party

at Global Wildlife, a wildlife refuge with literally hundreds of acres
filled with zebras, giraffes, camels, deer, and kangaroos. Visitors
experience the animals up close on safari wagon rides. Because of
all this, we decided that Global Wildlife would be the place for the
party.

In the midst of prepping for his upcoming birthday party, I felt
a bit nostalgic and wanted to put my mind in a different direction. I
decided to organize baby pictures.

As I thumbed through piles of pictures, memories played through
my mind of the times they were taken. Some of the most special
pictures to me were always the ones of my boys with their grandparents. Seeing them with my parents and Billy's parents always made
me smile because I know how precious that will be to them one day.
I never had a chance to sit in my grandfather's lap because he passed
before I was born. And the memories I have of my grandmother are
the most precious and valued of them all. When I was fourteen years
old, God called her home, and I have missed her dearly since then. I
often thought of how she would smile at my own children and how
proud she would be of the great kids they are.

I spent more time reminiscing through Matthew's and Conner's pictures than actually trying to organize them into scrapbooks like I originally intended. As I went deeper into the pile, I began to realize that we did not have one single picture of our extended family anywhere in our home. I realized that there were even fewer of our immediate family since moving into the house and this wasn't right.

I thought deeper about just who was missing and made mental notes about the pictures I wanted to round up. One of the first ones I thought of was my grandparents. Over the past couple of months I had thought of my grandmother Opal Massey numerous times. I didn't really know why; I just knew that I had found comfort in thinking about Grandma Massey while Matthew was sick. Having a picture of my maternal grandparents was something I needed to work on.

I knew my mom had some pictures of them in some old albums because I remembered seeing them as a child, but I had not seen those pictures in years. It had been quite some time since I spent an afternoon flipping through her albums. I wanted to get at least one picture of them to put up in my office.

One of the pictures that always stood out as a favorite was one that was on a slide. It was a picture of my grandparents, Grandma Massey and Pop Massey, in their front yard taken for their fiftieth wedding anniversary. For whatever reason, I always loved seeing that picture when it would come up in the slide show. While my mind was on it, it should not be too difficult to go next door and see if I could locate the slide box with that particular image.

The photo project was something fun for me and after what had happened, it was a nice change to focus on something upbeat. I explained to my mom what I wanted to do. She led me to the spare room where she kept the old boxes. We blew off the dust and found the box that was labeled with those slides. I thumbed through the round carousel until I found it. "There it is!" I was so happy. "This is the exact one that I was thinking of." Mom told me to go ahead and scan it to my computer. A few clicks of the mouse and there it was. I printed it out and placed the image high on a bookshelf in the office. It was exactly what I wanted.

The afternoon wore on, and it was getting close to the time that

Matthew needed to have his next blood pressure reading and medicine. I retrieved Matthew and Conner from my parents' house and returned the slide. Mom asked if it worked, and I assured her that the job was done, but I still needed a frame.

The boys and I returned home. We had an afternoon snack, and then Matthew had his next blood pressure reading. All was still stable. It was higher than it should be for his age, but it was stable given his condition. Matthew had his medicine, and the boys retreated to the living room to resume their playing with Hot Wheels. While they were content for a few minutes, I went back to the office to put away the picture project. Pictures were strewn all over my office desk and floor. With a sigh, I placed the piles of baby pictures neatly back into their respective albums and boxes.

Just as I was finishing up, I heard little feet coming down the hall toward the office. That sound always made me smile. From the spacing of the steps, I knew it was Matthew. He bounced into the office and with the sweetest tone said, "Hi, Mom! What are you doing?"

"Well, buddy, I went through some of your baby pictures today and now I am putting away my mess."

He just grinned. "That sounds like fun. Next time can I look too?"

"Of course you can. Maybe next week we can pull them all out." This seemed to satisfy him.

"Conner is probably missing me. I am going to go finish playing cars with him." Matthew walked close to where I was sitting and gave me the biggest, tightest hug ever. "Mom, I sure do love you!" Those words will make a mom's heart melt in an instant.

"I love you too, buddy! You and Conner have fun. Daddy will be home shortly, and we will have dinner."

With that he turned to bounce back out of the office. However, he stopped in his tracks mid turn. As he had headed back toward the door, his eye caught the top of my bookshelf. He stared at the picture I had placed up there earlier. With his eyes locked on it, he walked slowly toward the bookshelf.

In a quick motion he grabbed the picture from the shelf to get a better look at it. A look was on his face unlike any I have ever seen before.

With all of the seriousness he could muster, Matthew looked at me in disbelief and asked, "Who are these people?" His tone was slightly different from the happy, lively child who had come into the room a few minutes earlier. Taken aback by the change of demeanor, I wasn't sure what caused this sudden change.

"Matthew, those are my grandparents. Why do you ask?" As he stared at the picture, it begin to shake in his hand, and an unknown emotion had come over him like a tidal surge. "Matthew, what's wrong? This is just a picture of my grandparents, Grandma Massey and Pop Massey."

His stare finally broke and he looked up at me with complete confidence. "No, they're not! Those are not your grandparents. These are two of the angels who came to get me. Why do you have a picture of them? Where did you get it?" His voice was full of misunderstanding and wonder. He had never seen this image before and just didn't understand why it was in our home.

Matthew's reaction to this image was overwhelming. His tiny hands were trembling as they held the photo. He was not necessarily afraid but was utterly surprised to have a printed image of the "angels," as he called them, who had protected and comforted him. We had not mentioned or discussed what happened since he had first shared the experience with us. We trusted that he would talk about it again when he was comfortable. Well, that time of additional discussion was here!

eighteen

AN ANGEL OF LOVE

I took a deep breath while gathering up all of the thoughts that were swirling around. Billy and I already agreed to make sure that Matthew knew we supported him and would listen with an open mind and heart anytime he wanted to discuss it. Honestly, at this point in time, we didn't know if Matthew would ever mention it again. I prayed for God to give me understanding and direction to help Matthew. Even praying this request to God, I still didn't fully trust in how he could ever give me the ability to help my little boy understand something that I didn't fully comprehend. All I could do was keep asking for his help in getting over this mountain in our lives. I had to trust that God had this under control.

After a few seconds, I asked Matthew to come sit with me. Still staring intently at the picture, he landed in my lap, and we looked at it together. This image that had always conjured up a happy emotion for me now was the source of great question for my little boy. His little hands were trembling less. I kissed the side of his head gently and whispered in his ear that it was okay. My arms were wrapped around him, so I could feel his little heart. A rapid heartbeat could be a serious issue for a hypertensive child. I wanted to feel his chest to make sure his heart was slowing down. Softly I whispered in his ear, "Okay, buddy, let's take a few deep breaths." In unison the breaths would come slow and deep until all was settled. "Matthew, tell Mommy exactly who the people in the picture are." After a few seconds, he quietly explained, "Mom, these are two of the angels that I walked with when I was going to heaven."

As he pointed to my grandmother, he said, "This lady is who met me and put her hand out to me. She is the person I talked to."

Still trying to choose my words correctly, "Baby, I remember you saying to me and Dad that you did talk to one of the angels. Can you tell me again what you said to each other?" I had remembered exactly what he told us only a few weeks earlier. Asking him to tell me again would give me an opportunity to see if there was any variation from the original account.

As his little finger rubbed across the image of my grandmother, he once again shared: "This lady reached out her hand to me and said it was time for me to go with them. There were two men and two women. I told her that I could not go with her because I had not asked my mom and dad. This lady told me that it was okay because you knew I would be going and I should come with her. She made me feel safe and I wasn't scared." So far, this was the same vision he described before. "I was standing in the middle of these two people, and they held my hands," he explained as he picked up the picture to bring it closer to my face to show me. "The lady looked down at me and asked if I was ready and I said yes. We just started walking."

Even though we had not doubted any aspect of his original story, he had once again just given validity to this entire experience by sharing it word for word again, weeks later. From his reaction to the picture and the emotion he showed, this was something that had obviously impacted him deeper than we had originally thought. After he sat for a little while, he turned and looked up at me with tears and a smile and asked, "Mom, you really know my angels?"

Utter happiness and relief had replaced the earlier reaction of confusion. I explained, "Well, I know the lady. Her name was Opal

Massey, but we called her Grandma Massey. I knew her until she passed away when I was fourteen years old. I never met my grandfather, Pop Massey. He passed away before I was born." The thought flashed instantly of how many times I had dreamt of my grandmother knowing and seeing my boys. At that moment, I was elated because the one person I wanted to meet my children had not only protected Matthew but also had been the single most significant source of comfort for his entire little

Opal and Noah Massey

life when he needed it most. "Matthew, are you absolutely sure these are the people you saw?" I asked.

"Yes, Mom, I am positive!" he explained without hesitation or doubt. "I have held hands with these two people." Still looking at me, "Mom, I can't believe you know her too! The man did not say anything to me. We did not talk. He just held my hand tight, but the lady was so nice."

Processing this was difficult to say the least. "Matthew, you met Grandma Massey!"

It had always been my understanding that in some way after we pass on, we will be reunited with those whom we loved that went before us. Matthew affirmed this belief for me.

I asked, "Baby, do you have any idea who the other two 'angels' were?"

Shaking his head back and forth, "No, Mom. I don't know them. I have never seen them. I didn't think I knew the first two either until today." To this day it remains a mystery who the other man and woman were that gave peace to Matthew on that short walk.

Hugging Matthew tightly and stroking his little head as he lay against my chest was such a peaceful feeling. I asked Matthew if he had any questions or anything else he wanted to talk about. "Mom, do you think these people are living with Jesus, and one day we will live there too?" Again, this was one of those questions that a parent can't give a yes or no answer to.

Matthew continued on, "Mommy, it was so beautiful in heaven."

As I peered down at this little guy in my lap, I asked, "Matthew, how did you know it was heaven?"

A smile came over his face and he said, "There is nowhere that would have as much love and be as pretty as heaven. Everything was white. The angels wore white robes and they were all white, except that I could see their faces."

I continued to look at him in amazement, trying to comprehend the words coming from his mouth. This little boy's eyes had seen so much majesty.

Matthew asked, "Mommy, are you sure you're not mad that I didn't want to come back?"

The only thing I could do was hug him so tightly that he knew my love. I thought the whole parenting thing was going to get easier after they were potty-trained and did not need bottles. Boy, was I wrong! I have learned something new every day about other human beings, especially children, since giving birth to Matthew. Sometimes I chuckle and think, *Boy, does God have a sense of humor when it comes to the curveballs he pitches to parents of little ones!*

nineteen

TAKE NOTHING FOR GRANTED

After the boys were tucked into bed, I shared the day's events with Billy. The expression on his face revealed every emotion I had in my heart earlier in the day. It was more confirmation to me of all that had happened and how close Matthew came to no longer being with us. That night was a pivotal point in our relationship as a couple and as parents. The past couple of months had really taught us not to take for granted even the smallest of things each day. But for some unknown reason, after what had been revealed to us by our precious little boy, we turned a complete about-face and truly started putting the important things into perspective.

I think this was a unique turning point in deepening our faith and our trust in God and his power and mercy. Always being Christians, we never really had that earth shattering, powerful, epiphany of really seeing God's divine grace and the things at play beyond our control as humans. We knew it was there but kind of rolled through our days robotically never really feeling it. We sat

Grandma and Pop Massey

in silence and looked at each other shaking our heads. We were trying to make sense of everything.

All of this was not a bad thing. It was a truly positive thing. First, we still had our son with us. After all, we had just had the chance to tuck him into bed another night. Second, we have had a rare insight into what is to come for each of us after we pass away from this earth and God calls us each home. Not many people have this precious gift. And because of this insight we could as a family use it as away to make every day count for the rest of our lives on earth.

No doubt this experience changed Matthew in some of the most profound ways imaginable. Some might hesitate to believe that a child so young could have such a powerful experience and be able to recall with such eloquence and simplicity the beauty that he experienced. Well, those skeptics have never met Matthew. Billy and I knew that our lives were changed forever, and we were happy to meet the challenge.

Our lives were changed. We were raising a child who had a glimpse of what awaits all of us. It was important that Matthew knew we supported him and would help him continue to heal and understand. We could take this experience and miss the important message that God was sharing with us as a family, or we could learn from it and become more fervent Christians. We chose the latter.

There were still many dark days ahead for Matthew and his health issues, and we knew that we would never endure it through them without our faith and the love of God and a true belief that he hears all prayers.

I shared the experience with the picture and Matthew's conversation with my mom and my sister because I really just needed support from them and an ear to listen to me. As always, they met this with all of the love and understanding imaginable.

Matthew was drawn into such a deep realization that God's love is amazing. And to have witnessed with his own eyes what many people have debated and discussed made him mature and grow so much. He had always been a thoughtful child and had always had a maturity beyond his years, and this circumstance fostered those traits.

As time went on, Matthew spoke often of "his time with the angels" as he referred to it. Billy and I agreed that if and when it was brought up, he would not be shunned. Different things on occasion would remind him, and he would talk about it. Never once straying from the first time he spoke of it, our family knew that Matthew had an amazing journey on a brief walk with four angels who gave him peace—so much peace that he didn't want to return—and comfort and allowed him safety at a horrible time. As Matthew continued to grow and time passed, we were presented with more challenges that would test our faith again.

twenty

TIME FOR SCHOOL

The summer of 2007 was quiet in our new routine of diet restrictions, activity restrictions, frequent hydration, round-the-clock blood pressure checks, and medicines. Matthew and Conner continued to grow closer and closer, becoming best friends. Matthew will never have a bigger supporter, cheerleader, or prayer partner than his little brother. Conner was faced with unimaginable challenges that only the sibling of a chronically ill child can ever relate to. He constantly faced the possibility of his big brother being in the hospital for days or weeks at a time and his family being disrupted by this.

With all of the emotion that goes into this scenario, Conner was tremendously mature in understanding when Matthew couldn't play anymore or he needed to stop and take medicine. If anything, he was always the one asking Matthew if he needed a break. He never once complained and would often rest with Matthew. This characteristic has not wavered in the years they have grown. As a mom, it makes me so proud to see that kind of God-given compassion for another human being. In some instances a sibling of a chronically ill brother or sister can become resentful or disgruntled. Not Conner.

The fall of 2007 rolled around, and it was time to start kindergarten. After the events of Matthew's little life and the experiences he had, we felt it was important that Matthew go to a school where he could openly and freely discuss his love of God and his understanding of God's power. We decided to enroll Matthew at a Christian, faith-based elementary school, similar to the mission of the church and preschool he attended when he had been ill. Enrolling Matthew at Parkview was the best decision and biggest sacrifice we ever made. He was blessed to be surrounded by the most amazing Christian teachers, faculty, and staff who embraced him with love and nurturing that allowed him to shine academically and personally.

The health issues and daily routines became second nature to all of us, and we lived as normal a life as possible. Communication was key to all of our healing, and we spoke openly and often about what each of us was feeling. Not that we looked for answers, but just expressing our feelings made a huge difference. Matthew talked about nearly dying just like any other child would talk about going to Disney World. This was a part of his life, and it was not something he was ashamed of. His faith in God grew more and more as time went on. His understanding of scripture as it has been taught to him over the years is amazing. It seems like when you have a personal stake in something, it becomes more interesting to you and you develop a more personal interest.

Pop and Grandma Massey on their fiftieth wedding anniversary

Kindergarten went well, and he managed to

finish the year strong. He looked forward to first grade, and we knew it would be another exciting year for him. The school year started and he was off to a great start. We continued his daily routine of medications and blood pressure monitoring, but it was a manageable rigor.

Then in early November I got a call from his teacher saying that he had a headache, and it seemed to be different from the sometimes "usual" side effect headaches he would get. I ran to school with his blood pressure machine. His blood pressure was around 145 systolic even with three different medications, which was worrisome. I signed him out, and we headed home to call the doctor and see what we needed to do.

After a quick call to his nephrologist, we were advised to pack a bag and get him to Children's as soon as possible. The tears instantly started pouring down my face as the nurse said this was what he had been fearing for the past year and a half. The temporary fix of the balloon angioplasty had come to an end, and it was time to reevaluate. It was a very emotional time for us as we packed up once again. Saying good-bye to Conner was very difficult. Billy's own father was still in the hospital after having surgery for colon cancer, so it was hard for us to leave Billy's parents at such a hard time for them. But we had no control over this situation, and Matthew had to get better.

In the blink of an eye, we were in New Orleans, and Matthew was being triaged in the ER. He was put into a room in no time, and the game plan was to have another angiogram to evaluate his condition. His blood pressure was beginning to rise to critical levels again, and the medications were no longer controlling the pressures safely. The procedure was scheduled for the following morning. Not being able to control any aspect of what was going on, all we could do was turn it over to God.

Matthew's nephrologist was present during the angiogram with the radiologist. After it was complete, they came into the waiting room to bring us the news. It was not good. The blocked artery that had temporarily been repaired needed major surgical intervention. Additionally, some aneurysms were found in the renal artery structure. Two blockages were found on the right side that were not previously known. Not only were we now faced with having to find a solution to fix the major issue on the left side, but also we began to worry about the right side.

As if we needed it, we had another gut-wrenching blow that tested our faith. Since Matthew's health issues started a year and a half earlier, it was our understanding that when the time came for more intervention to fix the left side, he would just have bypass surgery—the surgery that he was not strong enough for at four and a half years old. However, this was not an option now.

Due to the structure and anatomy of the aneurysms and the renal artery, we needed to explore other options. Matthew's nephrologist recommended that we consult with a transplant surgeon. Transplant? Naturally this scared us.

We came home with instructions to keep Matthew as calm as possible and limit is activity because his blood pressure was erratic. We went back the following week to meet with the transplant surgeon. He instantly gained our confidence and trust, just like we had trusted Matthew's nephrologist. This was our son's life we were talking about, and we needed to have confidence in the doctor's abilities and his vested interest. After a blood pressure reading from all four quadrants of the heart, the surgeon explained to us that he had reviewed Matthew's file extensively. He knew everything that had gone on with him since March 2007.

After looking at the latest angiogram findings, the doctor made two suggestions. The first was to do a nephrectomy and completely remove his left kidney. People live with one kidney all the time. However, in Matthew's case, we now knew that his right kidney had two smaller blockages that could become an issue in the future. If they do, then he would be left with no working kidneys, and that meant dialysis and waiting for a donor organ.

The second option was a fairly unheard-of procedure at the time called an auto kidney transplant. This invasive surgery would remove his left kidney, repair the blocked portion of the artery, and transplant the kidney back into the pelvis if it was found to be healthy and viable enough to do so. The doctor was honest and said that at that time he had only performed it on a couple of adult patients. He had already discussed his recommendations with the nephrologists, but the decision was up to us as to what to do. Our heads were spinning. The doctor could give no guarantees with either procedure. He changed from being a doctor to being a "real" person at that moment. He calmly explained that something has to be done in order to save Matthew's life. The only decision to make was which surgical procedure to move forward with. He added that if it were his son and he was facing the same situation, he would opt to have the auto transplant done and take a chance that the left kidney was still viable. If not, we were left with a worst-case scenario: a nephroctomy is done and his right kidney stops working in the future. This was a lot to take in. The doctor asked us to go home and discuss it. He said to call him with any questions and then we would meet again in a couple of days and map out a plan.

Matthew was calm as we left. He had listened to every word. As we sat down to eat some lunch on the way back home, Billy and I were tense. We were still trying to wrap our heads around a decision that could impact our child's life in ways that we couldn't or didn't want to comprehend. How were we faced with such a difficult task again for this innocent child? The waitress brought our waters to the table, and I looked at Matthew, who was sitting quietly.

"Matthew, of course this decision is not yours to make, but you have known every aspect of what has happened to you medically. If it were up to you, what would you do?"

He looked at Billy and me and, with the calmest expression, he said, "Well, Mom, you heard the doctor. It's really a no-brainer. If they take my left kidney and my right kidney stops working, then that's bad. But, if we try the auto transplant and it works, then that's best. If we don't try, we will never know." The words coming out of a six-year-old's mouth had all the wisdom of a person four times his age. His dad and I agreed with what he was saying and told him that we would make a decision later after some prayerful consideration.

That night we sat down once again to go over options. We kept coming back to what was clearly the best option. We prayed over it and knew in our hearts that the best thing for Matthew

Matthew and Dad, December 22, 2008

would be to attempt the auto transplant. We drove back to Children's Hospital in a couple of days for our follow-up to let the doctor know our decision. When we arrived for our appointment, the surgeon had been called into an emergency liver transplant because an organ had become available for a small child during the night. He was able to take a break and made a call from the operating room to a conference room we were waiting in. I told him our decision, and he said that we could either wait until just before or after Christmas. This was the second week of December. Billy and I had already thrown around options for when to do the surgery in coordination with the surgeons schedule. We could not put off the surgery any longer.

By this point, Matthew was unable to even go to the bathroom without me carrying him because his blood pressure would spike, and he had constant headaches and dizziness. I remember telling the surgeon that we were willing to give up one Christmas to have a lifetime of Christmases with Matthew. This was probably the easiest decision we had to make. It was something that as a family we knew just had to be done. We can celebrate the birth of Jesus anywhere, including a hospital, if need be. As a mom, though, my heart was heavy knowing that Conner and Matthew would be making a huge sacrifice in giving up the joy of a child at Christmas. We knew God would make this all work out.

Surgery was scheduled for December 23, 2008. We had to check in the day before. The surgeon personally brought in all of the consent forms and went over the risks and complications with us in detail. I could feel God's presence as I signed that paper. I had no hesitation or doubt. I trusted each and every one of the doctors and knew God would see Matthew through.

Our evening was filled with a lot of laughter and prayer, and a serene, calm feeling permeated that room. The surgery had to be done, and we needed to face it with that resolve. To our surprise and elation, we were joined that evening for a few brief minutes by a special person from Matthew's school. Mrs. Martha Long was head of the ele-

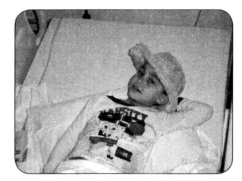

Matthew, December 22, 2008

mentary division and worked closely with Matthew and his teachers to keep his academic studies up to date while he was in and out of the hospital. She drove nearly two hours in her free time to come pray with us the night before surgery. We were so overwhelmed with her kind commitment to one of her students. After a few minutes of visiting and an amazing prayer led by Mrs. Long, she was on her way.

We enjoyed some dinner and a movie, and then it was lights out to get some rest before the big day. The last thing I did before going to sleep was the same as it had been every night before. Pray, pray, pray for God to heal Matthew and lift him up from all of this strife in his young life. I prayed for him to be brave and to know the enormous love that was felt from everyone. And with that, I attempted to rest a few hours before the surgery.

twenty-one

LITTLE BEAN

Six in the morning came early and the first person in the hospital room was one of the surgical residents. He gave some preliminary information for us to digest as far as timing of how things would go that morning. By six thirty the nurses were giving Matthew his least-favorite substance on the planet: Versed. The taste was unpleasant, and the feeling of losing control as his body relaxed was not something that he enjoyed.

He lifted the tiny medicine cup to his nose for a whiff, and nothing in that liquid appealed to his sense of smell. But, after some coaxing, he was determined and knew it had to be done. Like the champion he is, he bravely swallowed it. The clock said six forty-five, and one of the techs from surgery was at the door to get him. This was it.

Once again, I silently asked God to be with our baby as he to embarked on one of the scariest, uncertain events of his little life. Knowing that we would be not coming back to the sixth floor for a while, we gathered our bags in our arms and slowly meandered out the door. Matthew would need to be in the PICU for some time following the major surgery. Hearing the door close behind us was a poignant sound. It marked the end of one battle, but we were being led into an entirely new and unsure voyage.

All of the laughter and calm from the night before had now given way to nerves and uneasiness. Billy and I were anxious thinking of all the things that could go wrong. The worst-case scenario would be if the kidney was too damaged to be transplanted and he had to have the nephrectomy anyway. Prayers were constant for the kidney to be viable and healthy.

By the time we got into the surgical prep area, he was good and loopy. Matthew looked up and smiled, "Hey, Mom, you have one huge eyebrow! Not two anymore. Just one that goes all the way across your head." He just giggled. I am so glad that I had that silly laugh to replay in my head during the next few hours. Not tears, just his sweet little laugh. We kissed him and said a prayer, asking God to once again lift him up and carry him through. We then left him to the care of the surgery team anxiously waiting for him.

As we exited to the waiting room, Billy was relieved to see his youngest brother, Kurt, in the waiting area. He had driven to New Orleans to sit with us and offer support during surgery. Billy's nerves were frayed, and it was good to have someone besides me to pass the time. A few minutes later we were joined by our church pastor, Pastor Kim Little-Brooks. As soon as she got there, we joined hands and prayed for complete success and healing and prayed for the doctor's skilled hands to make Matthew better. We knew that science, intelligence, and education were on their side, and we could not have possibly had a better team of doctors.

As we settled into the nervous, meaningless conversations to pass the time, I pondered Matthew's visit with the angels. He had said that my grandmother said to him, "I will see you again someday." Would December 23, 2008, be that "someday?" Every effort was made to push that thought as far from my mind as possible and focus on the healing that God would provide. We hoped that "someday" would not come until he was old and gray and had lived a life full of goodness and favor.

The minutes passed slowly; it felt like an eternity as we waited for word on Matthew's progress and condition. My anxiety level was high. My heart was racing and my palms were sweating. We sent some quick text messages to let everyone at home know that there was still no word. I wanted to cry just because I felt so helpless.

However, I needed to find some positive emotion and stay focused. I petitioned God to calm me. I silently cried out to him to help me find this peace and calm, so I could be totally focused on helping Matthew when he came out of surgery. At that moment I was flooded with chilled air for just a few seconds; it was like the wind rushing by as a car passes someone waiting on the corner of a busy street. A complete blanket of peace washed over me. To put my feelings into words is difficult because the feeling streaming through me was nearly indescribable. I had no doubt that God knew the moment of weakness that I was in, and his divine power listened to my needs.

I offered up my gratitude, and my mind immediately replayed the life-changing revelation Matthew had shared with us. The powerful meaning of that near-passage into heaven was a source of comfort to me at that moment. I felt peaceful, thinking of the glorious sights he had seen, and his hands being cradled by the very woman who had cradled me when I was a baby. Whenever I had taken the time to ponder what it all meant, I was swept with sorrow.

But, for some reason, this time was different. My eyes again filled with tears, but not of grief. They were tears of gratitude. I knew that during this difficult time when we couldn't physically be with Matthew, he was cared for by something much more powerful than just the amazing surgeons. God's army of angels were in full force watching over Matthew and ensuring his protection. No matter what, he was not alone. And because of his path into the opening realm of heaven months before, Matthew was not afraid.

Why would I find peace and comfort in knowing that my son almost died? My comfort did not come from the thought of his near death. The peace was knowing that every day God and his angels were in us and through us to deliver on God's word to his people. Tranquility filled me, and I knew that my children would never walk alone. Our faith and the firsthand account we were privileged to hear from Matthew allowed me to see that something more majestic awaits each of us when we pass from this world. The moving, honest words of our Matthew opened my heart to view the world with different eyes

About an hour and a half into surgery, the nurse came into the waiting room and said the kidney was out, and the doctors were working to fix the blockage in his artery. A donor artery was made available if it was needed. The kidney looked good, and the surgeon thought it was viable to be transplanted back. It was considerably smaller due to the long-term restricted blood flow, but the surgeon was confident it could be saved.

Another hour went by and we saw the nurse again, bringing more good news. The kidney was back in and was nice and pink. Now all we waited for was to hear the last words that would be pivotal to the success of this operation. Another half hour later she again emerged, saying, "The kidney is making urine!" There were collective sighs of relief and happy tears. Never in my life would I have imagined that I would be so elated to hear those words.

The surgery took a little under four hours. Once I knew the doctors were finishing up and everything was good, I sent out my chain of text messages to let everyone know the good progress. After a while I ran to the cafeteria to get an apple juice. I knew that once he went to the PICU, I needed to be at the door ready to go in as soon as Matthew was prepped.

On my way back to the waiting room, I actually passed the surgery team with Matthew's bed being transferred to the PICU. Matthew was lost under the maze of wires, tubes, leads, IVs, and blankets. His face was still puffy, even more so now. As his kidney function had slowed in the past weeks, he had some pretty significant swelling because fluid was being retained. I knew, though, that God had heard our prayers and Matthew was moving in the right direction. It was going to be a long road, but it was a road leading to great things. I ran back to the waiting room and told Billy I had seen our son. We all made our way to the PICU waiting area to await the call to go in. By this time, we were joined by Billy's uncle Randy and aunt Lauri. They were there to offer support and love, as always.

It felt like we waited an eternity to go see Matthew. My need to hold my baby's hand was paramount. I needed to be at his side. The anxiety of wanting to see what his blood pressure readings was all- consuming. We had lived by numbers for the past year and a half. Even though we were told that this surgery may not totally bring his blood pressure back to normal, we had prayed constantly for this to be the case. We assumed that he would need some type of maintenance dose of blood pressure medication for the rest of his life. Only time would tell. But I trusted God had everything under control.

Finally, a nurse said we could go in. Matthew was still heavily sedated and would probably stay that way through the night. He had just been cut from as far down as one can imagine to the middle of his chest. Everything in his abdominal cavity had been pushed, prodded, and rearranged to make room for the new neighbor, "Little Bean"—this was the name given to his kidney after it was transplanted. We knew that the sedation and medications would take some time, but we were patient.

Once everyone knew that he was okay, Billy's family left. Then we had another welcome visit from my cousin Daimon, who had recently moved to New Orleans with his family. The love and support of our families was such a blessing. God has a way of knowing exactly what we needed, when we needed it. Daimon dropped by to check on everyone and make sure we were doing well. It was a welcome visit, and I was thankful to see him.

After the first hour of Matthew being in the PICU, everyone had left except for me and Billy. Now to do what we had come so accustomed to: sit, watch, and wait. At the time, the PICU was in a temporary location and was not built with comfort in mind. The rooms were designed for life-saving and healing measures. There was one rolling chair beside the bed—a tiny, hard, straight-backed chair. We agreed that we would alternate the afternoon (meaning we would both be in the room because I wasn't about to leave him). I

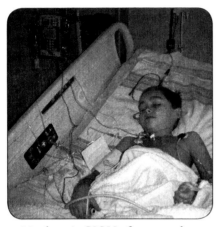
Matthew in PICU after transplant

would stay for the night shift, and Billy would stay in the morning. During my time in the room, Billy would stay in the PICU lounge. This was not exactly somewhere you feel safe actually going to sleep with your belongings.

The initial numbers for his blood pressure were not what I was excited to see. But I reminded myself that it was not a true assessment yet. Matthew was in a lot of pain and had numerous medications on board.

We spent the afternoon watching Matthew and continuing to send up our silent prayers. We did not use our phones or turn on the TV so there would be nothing to disturb him. With each visit from his nurse, we were told he was doing great and all of his vitals were stable. He remained sedated all afternoon and into the night. Only one person was allowed to be bedside at night, so I stayed with Matthew as Billy walked around the courtyard. I just sat and stared at him all night. I watched his monitor and saw every shift of his eyes behind his eyelids. At one point, I looked toward the window, and Billy was standing outside peering in just to be sure we were okay. Of course, if anything was not okay, he would have been the first to know. That was Billy's way of being with us even from a distance.

I had so many mixed emotions watching Matthew lay there struggling to recover—elation and gratitude at the miracle God allowed to happen again in the rare surgery, of course, but also deep, scorching pain to see my son hurting so much. He had indeed successfully made it through surgery, but he had a long road of recovery. Many uncertainties would still have to play out. As I observed Matthew's frail body like I had done so many nights before, I couldn't help but wonder if he would have another vision to share like he did a year and a half earlier. My prayer was that he wouldn't. I hoped he would not remember anything that had transpired the past twenty-four hours.

The night wore on, and there was not much change. Matthew remained heavily sedated and didn't move an inch. There were so many wires and tubes, and he had his IV ports and an NG tube along with the leads for all of his monitors. His vitals were being watched extremely closely. Most important, his blood pressure, as well as his heart rate, oxygen saturation, and temperature, was being watched.

By six thirty the next morning, it was time for shift change. As the nurses prepared for the day shift, I left the PICU to give Billy a rundown on the night. Not much to tell except Matthew's blood pressure was still erratic and high most of the time.

I needed to close my eyes if just for a few minutes, but knew I would not be able to in the waiting room. I found a bathroom down the hall and brushed my teeth and washed my face. Then I went into the parking lot and jumped into the backseat of my SUV. The back was packed with Matthew's Christmas gifts from Santa. We would bring Christmas to him if he couldn't be at home. It would not be the same, but it would still be something.

After rolling up my jacket for a pillow, I slept for about an hour and a half. When I woke up, it took me a minute to get my bearings and figure out what time it was. I would probably say that between taking care of teeth brushing and face washing in a public hospital bathroom and sleeping in the parking lot, I was at a new low in our

hospital experiences. Not one to complain, I was still grateful that God had seen Matthew through surgery safely, and we were happy to endure any discomfort necessary.

No sleep came to me, just a brief period of lying in silence listening to the busy parking lot. After I

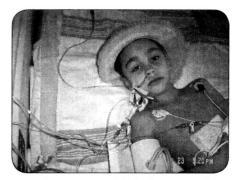

Matthew wearing his lucky orange hat

regrouped, I returned to the PICU, and Billy went out to rest for a bit. The morning went by at a turtle's pace, and eventually one of Matthew's surgeons and someone from nephrology came, rounded by a large team of residents. They were intrigued like a biology class dissecting a frog at what had been done to Matthew the day before. His vitals and postsurgical report were reviewed with enthusiasm. His doctors were happy to relay good news that even though it would be a long road ahead for him and he was still in the early stages of recovery, he appeared to be stable.

We were assured that if he remained in this condition, later in the evening we could possibly be in a regular room on the sixth floor. He would continue to be monitored with extreme caution from the nursing staff. But it would beat being in the PICU on Christmas Eve night. Around six that evening, we got the fantastic news he could go upstairs. He had finally opened his eyes a little earlier in the afternoon, and this was progress. The tube down his throat had been removed and he was attempting to speak a word or two.

The process to get him from the bed to the chair was agonizing. Even through the heavy pain meds, intense pain appeared on his face as we went upstairs. It had been less than forty-eight hours since his surgery, but in the sleep-deprived, nerve-racked emotional state we were, it may have well been forty-eight years. This was by far the most out-of-the-ordinary Christmas Eve in our lives. But with the chaos and worry of a sick child there was still many reasons for us to give thanks and say, "Happy birthday" to Jesus.

This Christmas instilled in us what Christmas is really about. It's not about the family traditions, the gifts, or the meals. It is celebrating the birth of our Savior, Jesus Christ, the one who was born, lived, and served to die on the cross for all of our sins. It was still painful to be separated from our family, and I enjoy all of the Christmas traditions we share with our family each year. It was sad to not participate in our annual Christmas Eve barbecue. This was just a small personal sacrifice to ensure that we would have many years of celebrations that would include Matthew. And it makes me think about God watching his own son suffer and allowing him to go through that pain for us when we really do not deserve it. God, with his amazing love for us, allowed his son to be sacrificed, and I was given my son back.

twenty-two

VISIT FROM SANTA

Once we got to room 613, we saw that Matthew's little Christmas tree was placed on his tray table. He was settled into bed, and I prayed for a good night's rest. Once we were settled upstairs, Billy made the mad dash to drive the two hours back home to spend Christmas Eve and Christmas morning with Conner. If we couldn't be together as a family, at least Billy could be with him. We said our good-byes and off he went. I prayed for God to guide him safely home and help him while he tried to juggle physically being at home to care for Conner but emotionally being at the hospital with Matthew. After Matthew was finally sleeping, Santa paid a visit. All of his gifts had been stored in the nurses' conference room when we arrived upstairs. After Santa came, the gifts were placed under Matthew's tree in hopes that it would bring a smile to his face the next morning.

It was clear there would be a lot of sacrifices for this surgery to happen during Christmas, but I had no idea that I would get to meet a real Santa. To my surprise, around midnight a gentle knock

Christmas at Children's, 2008

sounded on Matthew's door. When I opened it, one of the kindest men I've ever met was standing there. He quietly explained that he was a hospital volunteer, and they were bringing gifts to all of the patient rooms, so each child would have presents on Christmas morning. We were fortunate enough to know ahead of time we would be there and could plan accordingly, but so many patients and families didn't have that luxury. Tears started pouring down my face, and I could barely speak. The man was so polite and apologized if he had upset me.

Once I gained my composure, I had to explain to him that I was so moved and touched by this gesture that it overwhelmed me to know what generous souls walk among us. This was such a blessing, not because of the gifts but because these people sacrificed their time on such a treasured holiday to give to those who must be hospitalized. So many tireless people dedicate and volunteer to ensure that even sick children realize the joy of the season, and the hospital is quite a jubilant place to be in many aspects. Hospitals don't close just because it's Christmas, and kids don't stop getting sick. The work must go on. But God has used the gifts of time and the talents of so many to be missionaries to help these children during these special days.

Christmas Day came and went. We spent the day with Nanny Mel, Matthew and Conner's grandma, who made the drive to New Orleans, and Billy returned later in the afternoon after Conner had enjoyed his morning the best he could. During the next couple of days Nanny Dawn spent a day with him, and Mr. Raymond, our family friend, stopped by to bring him a special gift to cheer him up. It was an extremely long and agonizing week of meeting the necessary milestones to move toward discharge. In order for Matthew to be discharged, he had to be able to walk down the hall and around the nurses' station. This was a painful task, but he was determined to heal. His pain was off the charts, and there were some pretty serious side effects of some medications. Through it all, he worked really hard to get well enough to go home, which happened by New Year's Eve.

The next few months were filled with a lot of recovery and healing. Within a few weeks of surgery, Matthew was back at his schoolwork on a homebound basis, thanks to his aunt Mandy, who was willing to sacrifice her time to help him. She would administer his lessons and tests at home so he could keep pace with his class. The administrators and his teacher from school communicated closely to make sure that he got caught up and back on track. This work paid off because he returned to class in March and was exactly where he needed to be. He even managed to finish the year with straight As.

First grade was an exciting year, not in the typical sort of way, but in the God-filled blessing sort of way. During his recovery at home, Matthew continued to talk to us about his time with the angels and how peaceful it was. He found comfort in knowing that he has some special people watching out for him and knowing that God has great plans for his life. As first grade wound down, I took the time one afternoon to really praise him on the hard work and effort it took on his part to finish so strongly.

His reply to me was, "Mom, I didn't want to let

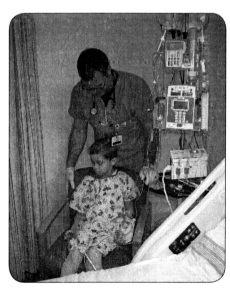

Christmas at Children's, 2008

Conner supporting his big brother

God down." This was such a powerful statement. After I asked why he had said that, he explained, "Well, God gave me a second chance to do good things on earth and I think doing well in school is one of those jobs." He has stood strong on those words and continues to excel academically, setting his bar higher each year.

The previous couple of years were a long, hard path for Matthew to travel, and unfortunately, it would not be the last in his list of hospitalizations and illnesses. Later in 2009, Matthew developed a complication from his transplantation surgery. Scar tissue had developed where his bladder and ureter were reattached and caused him to have a condition known as hydronephrosis. This caused urine to back up into his kidneys, which can be devastating if left untreated. Several more trips to the hospital finally led to an eighteen-day stay in the fall of that year and major surgery again to reimplant the ureter after removing the scar tissue.

During this time I gave serious thought to all that had transpired in our lives. There was the question of whether I could have done something different when I was pregnant to prevent this from happening or anything we could have done to have known how sick he was. I prayed for God to shed some light on these questions. I felt I was at a crossroads. Even though I was grateful that Matthew was still with us to keep fighting, I desired to find some answers. We had been told all along this was just a congenital condition. It just happened while he was in the womb. Nothing I could have

Mom and Matthew,
Tulane Hospital, 2009

done would have prevented this from happening.

I found some information that led me to think we could have identified this problem earlier than was realized. I began to research and realized that recommendations are in place for all children to have routine blood pressure screens beginning at age three. How-

Mom, Conner, and Matthew,
Tulane Hospital, 2009

ever, this is not the case in a lot of health care facilities, and this fact did not sit well with me. A blood pressure reading would not have changed what Matthew was born with, but it would have certainly allowed us to identify the condition nearly a year and a half earlier than it was found. This may not sound like a lot of time, but when you are talking about a child who was only four when he was diagnosed, this was nearly half of his life.

After some additional research and investigation into this matter, I realized this is not just an isolated issue or case. Nearly two million children in the United States suffer silently with undiagnosed and untreated hypertension. Undiagnosed because not all health care facilities do routine blood pressure screenings as is recommended.

Once Matthew was discharged from the hospital in the fall of

Celeste presenting on blood pressure
issues in children

2009, I called up one of my oldest and dearest friends, Monica. We have known each other since we were seventeen years old, and no one knows me better than she does. She knew all that Matthew had endured and was well aware of his struggles. I laid out all of the information that had been researched on

Matthew being interviewed for an
NPBPAF event

blood pressure issues in children and proposed we raise awareness to the issue. Before I could even finish she enthusiastically said, "I'm in! Whatever you need from me, I'll be there."

The groundwork started, and because of Matthew and his journey, we founded the National Pediatric Blood Pressure Awareness Foundation in January 2010. This is a national nonprofit organization that works to educate and advocate on the serious need for increased blood pressure screenings for all children beginning at age three. Matthew's suffering has not been in vain, and his faith and trust in knowing God has a great plan for his life is playing out every day as his story works to help other children and families. Lives are being saved because of Matthew's experience and the awareness being brought to this issue because of him. Matthew is outspoken on how important this cause is to him, and this diligent work has all allowed him to grow into the amazing boy he is now.

twenty-three

2013

Matthew has become the catalyst for invoking change and a symbol for what faith and miracles look like. Today Matthew is a healthy, vibrant young man who enjoyed his eleventh birthday in 2013. He keeps God first in every aspect of his life and enjoys spending as much time as possible with his little brother, Conner, and his friends. He is currently in middle school at the same school he has been in since kindergarten.

One of his favorite classes continues to be Bible study. He recently set a personal goal to read the entire Bible. His deep understanding of the words that were written thousands of years ago is amazing even to adults. As his mother, I could not be more proud of the young man he is becoming. He has aspirations of attending medical school to be a pediatric nephrologist. After all of his experiences and hospitalizations, he still wants to devote his life to helping others and giving back in the ways so much was given to him in the form of his health and life.

Matthew, age 11, and Conner, age 8

His connection to Christ is apparent to anyone who spends some time with him. Listening to him talk about the key players and stories of the Bible is riveting given his young age. His grasp of understanding is beyond his years. I have no doubt that his soul was touched and his life was enriched during those moments when he walked with the angels. Matthew has never taken for granted the experience or the meaning of having a second chance. Our family still openly talks about that experience. It marked each of us in ways that, I believe, have made us view things in a much more positive light. We don't take little things for granted.

We hope to provide an insight to anyone who is hurting or in need of healing after the loss of a loved one or facing saying good-bye to someone they care about. Part of the process is trying to understand what will happen to our loved ones when they pass on.

Even though we openly talk about Matthew's near-death experiences, I recently asked him to sit down with me and talk a little deeper about it. It has been some time since he shared the full story with me, and I asked him to again tell me what he remembered from that day.

Even at eleven years old, six years after his experience, his memory is still the same as it was when he was almost five. The description is the same, and now that he is older, he is able to expound even more in conveying the emotion of that day. I still cry each time I hear it. In fact, I rarely ever give a presentation without shedding a few tears. The emotion will probably always be raw. I still can't talk about something so deep and personal as my baby almost dying and not be emotional.

I asked him to tell me how this affected him now that he is older. With all of the wisdom of an older man, Matthew simply stated, "I am not afraid of death. I will never fear death; not now or when I am older because I know that when God calls me home, it will be all the beauty and grace that human words can't describe." He added, "Heaven is love. That is the feeling you have when you see the magnificent white glory of God's kingdom around you." His eyes will still fill with tears of understanding when he speaks of it. It is also a deep emotion for him but one that he shares in hope of helping others.

When I asked him his feelings on his story being shared, his response was simply, "If my story of almost dying can help others deal with a loss and let them know that they don't have to grieve out of fear of what happened to their loved one, then I will share it with everyone." What he shared with us as a family has now come full circle to help us understand what death means.

Matthew was not only able to help me answer this question by his account of spending time with my grandmother, but also at a time where we face the cycle of life and losing those that we love as they age, I am full of peace and gratitude. I'm grateful for each day God allows us so spend together in the time we have left on the earth, and I have peace in knowing that when our loved ones pass on, they will not go to a scary place, and they will not feel the sad emotions that we will. They will see love and beauty and will be greeted by those that they have loved and lost in their lifetime. The friends they have mourned and the family they have grieved will be there to welcome them into God's kingdom as they walk the path of white light into the arms of Jesus.

There will, of course, be sad tears for us when that time comes. But I can have reassurance that the mourning is for my personal loss, and I can rejoice in knowing that the grace of God will give them the peace and comfort to spend eternity in that beautiful kingdom, and I will one day see them again. I am so grateful to my son for being able to teach me a lesson that I never fully grasped in all of my years. No class or teacher could provide the same real insight as the one amazing four-year-old boy.

The Goodwin Family

A WORD FROM MATTHEW

My story, which is told in *A Boy Back from Heaven*, has forever changed my life. It has been six years since my journey started. I am now an eleven-year-old sixth-grader. My experience opened my eyes and taught me that heaven does exist, and it is a beautiful place. There is not an ounce of suffering, sickness, pain, and, best of all, there is no sin. I will never forget my journey. Because of it, I will never fear death. I know that death is just a rebirth. After rebirth you live in a miraculous place called heaven. When someone dies, I know they are going to feel better and have

Matthew, 2011

peace forever. I know that they are living with God.

My story has impacted many people's lives. Hopefully, my experience has given them a better understanding of heaven. In John 3:16 it is written, "For God so loved the world that he gave his one and only Son for whoever believes in Him shall not perish but have eternal life." I have been shown a glimpse of heaven, and I know that I will never die. Even after my body leaves this earth, I will go to heaven. I am appreciative that Christ died for us so that we have the privilege of going to heaven. My eyes have witnessed it, and I know how stunning it is. My illness has not been all negative. There have been many positives from being able to share my story, and I hope that it continues to help others.

2013

ABOUT THE AUTHOR

C ELESTE GOODWIN devotedly juggles her roles as an internationally sought Christian speaker, patient advocacy presenter in healthcare forums, national award-winning mom, wife, activist, and motivator. Celeste attributes her many successes to the values instilled by her parents, Rick and Evelyn. She grew up learning the value of hard work and what unconditional love was all about. When Celeste became a mother to Matthew and Conner, she settled into the routine many working moms do. She worked as a professional photographer and found balance between her husband, children, family, and home life. Then God's plan put Celeste on a different path and she became a mother helping her son fight for his life and keeping her family emotionally intact. Celeste discovered much about herself and the strength that can be pulled from places you never knew existed deep within your soul if you have faith. Her young son's health crisis brought her closer to God and gave her a deeper understanding and perspective of the importance of Christ in our lives and the unending love He shows to us. Celeste finds healing through sharing how powerful prayer can be.

As founder of the Baton Rouge–based nonprofit, National Pediatric Blood Pressure Awareness Foundation, Celeste devotes much of her time to the cause which she is passionate about. She is consistently educating and advocating on the issue of blood pressure in children and the need for increased screenings.

Celeste's husband, Billy, and their two children, Matthew and Conner are the beginning and end of her world and the motivation for all that she does. If you ask Celeste what her most important roles are, she will quickly tell you, child of Christ and being mom to Conner and Matthew. To learn more about Celeste and speaking engagements, please visit www.celestegoodwin.com. To learn more about NPBPAF, please visit www.bloodpressure4kids.org.